T0279737

DOROTHY DAY
Spiritual Writings

MODERN SPIRITUAL MASTERS

Robert Ellsberg, Series Editor

This series introduces the essential writing and vision of some of the great spiritual teachers of our time. While many of these figures are rooted in long-established traditions of spirituality, others have charted new, untested paths. In each case, however, they have engaged in a spiritual journey shaped by the challenges and concerns of our age. Together with the saints and witnesses of previous centuries, these modern spiritual masters may serve as guides and companions to a new generation of seekers.

Already Published

Modern Spiritual Masters (edited by Robert Ellsberg)
Swami Abhishiktananda (edited by Shirley du Boulay)
Metropolitan Anthony of Sourozh (edited by Gillian Crow)
Eberhard Arnold (edited by Johann Christoph Arnold)
Pedro Arrupe (edited by Kevin F. Burke, S.J.)
Daniel Berrigan (edited by John Dear)
Thomas Berry (edited by Mary Evelyn Tucker and John Grim)
Dietrich Bonhoeffer (edited by Robert Coles)
Robert McAfee Brown (edited by Paul Crowley)
Dom Helder Camara (edited by Francis McDonagh)
Carlo Carretto (edited by Robert Ellsberg)
G. K. Chesterton (edited by William Griffin)
Joan Chittister (edited by Mary Lou Kownacki and Mary Hembrow Snyder)
Yves Congar (edited by Paul Lakeland)
The Dalai Lama (edited by Thomas A. Forshoefel)
Dorothy Day (edited by Robert Ellsberg)
Alfred Delp, S.J. (introduction by Thomas Merton)
Catherine de Hueck Doherty (edited by David Meconi, S.J.)
Virgilio Elizondo (edited by Timothy Matovina)
Jacques Ellul (edited by Jacob E. Van Vleet)
Ralph Waldo Emerson (edited by Jon M. Sweeney)
Matthew Fox (edited by Charles Burack)
Charles de Foucauld (edited by Robert Ellsberg)
Mohandas Gandhi (edited by John Dear)
Bede Griffiths (edited by Thomas Matus)
Romano Guardini (edited by Robert A. Krieg)
Gustavo Gutiérrez (edited by Daniel G. Groody)
Thich Nhat Hanh (edited by Robert Ellsberg)

DOROTHY DAY

Spiritual Writings

Selected with an Introduction by
ROBERT ELLSBERG

ORBIS BOOKS

Maryknoll, New York 10545

The publishing arm of the Maryknoll Fathers and Brothers, Orbis seeks to explore the global dimensions of the Christian faith and mission, to invite dialogue with diverse cultures and religious traditions, and to serve the cause of reconciliation and peace. The books published reflect the views of their authors and do not represent the official position of the Maryknoll Society. To learn more, please visit our website at www.orbisbooks.com.

Grateful acknowledgment is made to Marquette University Press (Milwaukee, WI) for permission to include excerpts from *The Duty of Delight: The Diaries of Dorothy Day*, edited by Robert Ellsberg, copyright © 2008, *All the Way to Heaven: The Selected Letters of Dorothy Day*, edited by Robert Ellsberg, copyright © 2010. All rights reserved. www.marquette.edu/mupress. And thanks to Ave Maria Press for permission to use excerpts from Dorothy Day, *Thérèse*, copyright © 2015 (Notre Dame, IN). Excerpts from *The Long Loneliness* by Dorothy Day, copyright © 1952 by Harper & Row, Publishers, Inc., copyright renewed © 1980 by Tamar Teresa Hennessy, used by permission of HarperCollins, Publishers.

Manufactured in the United States of America

Library of Congress Cataloging-in-Publication Data

Names: Day, Dorothy, 1897-1980, author. I Ellsberg, Robert, 1955- editor.
Title: Dorothy Day : spiritual writings / Dorothy Day ; selected with an
    introduction by Robert Ellsberg.
Description: Maryknoll, NY : Orbis Books, [2024] I Series: Modern spiritual
    masters I Includes bibliographical references.
Identifiers: LCCN 2024017208 (print) I LCCN 2024017209 (ebook) I ISBN
    9781626985834 (trade paperback) I ISBN 9798888660386 (epub)
Subjects: LCSH: Day, Dorothy, 1897-1980. I Catholic converts. I Catholic
    Church—Charities. I Church and social problems.
Classification: LCC BX2182.3 .D393 2024 (print) I LCC BX2182.3 (ebook) I
    DDC 282—dc23/eng/20240618
LC record available at https://lccn.loc.gov/2024017208
LC ebook record available at https://lccn.loc.gov/2024017209

Contents

PREFACE

Dorothy Day's granddaughter, Kate Hennessy, has said that to have known Dorothy is to spend the rest of your life wondering what hit you. That is certainly the case for me. It is nearly fifty years since our first encounter, when, in 1975 at the age of nineteen, I took a leave from college, intending to spend a few months at the Catholic Worker. As it turned out, that short stay stretched into five years. I had only been at St. Joseph House a few months when Dorothy asked me to serve as managing editor of the newspaper, a task for which I had no evident qualifications.

Nevertheless, one of the first things I learned about Dorothy was her ability to recognize and encourage people's gifts and possibilities—possibilities, I should say, that weren't at all evident to ourselves. And so, in ways I could not have foreseen, she set me on the course of my life, much of it spent trying to understand what had hit me, and to share her story with the world.

Most of what I have come to understand about Dorothy Day has come from editing her writings, of which this volume is the sixth. I began to work on the first of these, *By Little and By Little: The Selected Writings of Dorothy Day*, soon after her death in 1980. Most recently I edited her *On Pilgrimage* columns from the 1960s and 1970s. But without a doubt I learned the most about her from the opportunity to edit her diaries and selected letters, *The Duty of Delight,* and *All the Way to Heaven.* From these volumes I learned in particular about the spirituality that was expressed in the ordinary events and encounters of her daily life.

Many people associate Dorothy Day with dramatic actions on the public stage—walking on picket lines; refusing to take shelter during compulsory civil defense drills during the 1950s; standing beside young men who were burning their draft cards during the Vietnam War; or being arrested at the age of seventy-five, while picketing with striking farmworkers in California.

From that final arrest, many are familiar with the famous photograph by Bob Fitch that shows her calmly sitting on a portable stool, offset by the outline of two burly, and well-armed police officers. It was that iconic image of "contemplation in action," as much as anything, that first attracted me to the Worker.

Of course, we also associate Dorothy with the daily work of the Catholic Worker—putting out a newspaper, living among the poor, practicing the works of mercy: feeding the hungry, sheltering the homeless, comforting the sorrowful and afflicted.

But reading and editing her diaries showed me that those activities were only the public face of a life that was mostly spent—as it is for all great souls, as well as the rest of us—in very ordinary and undramatic activities. And it was especially in that realm of ordinary daily life that she expressed her spirituality, and found her path to holiness.

Now, through her writings, and particularly the *Spiritual Writings* collected here, anyone can know Dorothy in this way. But still there are things about her that I think you could only know from spending time with her.

For one thing: her intense curiosity and interest in life.

Part of this came from the habits of a journalist, accustomed to carrying around a notebook to jot down facts and details about the places she went and the people she met. She never seemed bored or jaded. She was endlessly fascinated by other people—where they came from, what they had read, what they cared about. "What's your favorite novel by Dostoevsky?" she might ask. I think I told her *The Brothers Karamazov*—a book I had not actually read, though I was happy to learn that she agreed with me.

She had a great spirit of adventure. Always she seemed ready for something new, whether starting a house of hospitality for women, or standing up to the IRS when they took her to task for refusing to pay federal income taxes for war. When an exasperated IRS agent asked her to estimate how much she owed in taxes, she replied, "Why don't you tell me what you think I owe, and then I just won't pay it."

Regardless of how old she became, there was always a youthfulness to her. She loved the idealism and energy of young people, and what she called their "instinct for the heroic." She urged us to "aim for the impossible," noting that if we lowered our goal, we would also diminish our effort. Yet she was understanding of our mistakes and foibles. The memory of her own youthful struggles made her particularly sensitive to the searching and sufferings of youth.

She herself was always ready to be inspired and renewed. In her diary, she wrote, "No matter how old I get . . . no matter how feeble, short of breath, incapable of walking more than a few blocks . . . with all these symptoms of age and decrepitude, my heart can still leap for joy as I read and suddenly assent to some great truth enunciated by some great mind and heart."

For Dorothy, all of life was a school of charity and gratitude. Exercising the "duty of delight," she always seemed to look past the surface of things to another wider dimension. "There is desperate suffering with no prospect of relief," she wrote. "But we would be contributing to the misery and desperation of the world if we failed to rejoice in the sun, the moon, and the stars, in the rivers which surround this island on which we live, in the cool breezes of the bay, in what food we have and in the benefactors God sends us."

Dorothy was an avid collector of picture postcards, and some of them adorned the walls of her room at Maryhouse. They included icons and works of art, but also images from nature: forests, the ocean, polar bears. Dorothy spent most of her life surrounded by actual images of poverty, including the hungry men and women who waited outside the Catholic Worker each morning for a bowl of soup. But one of her most distinctive qualities was her sensitivity to beauty.

She delighted in the beauty of church or the Saturday afternoon opera on the radio. Yet she also noticed beauty in places that others might overlook: in a piece of driftwood, in the sound of a tanker on the Hudson, an ailanthus tree somehow clinging to life in the midst of a slum, the sunlight on the windows of a neighboring tenement building. But she also had an eye for moral beauty: the sight of someone sharing bread with a neighbor (the literal meaning of "companionship"). And hardest of all, she could see beauty where others did not, in the features of Jesus under the disguise of the poor and downtrodden.

She frequently quoted Dostoevsky's famous line, "The world will be saved by beauty." I often puzzled over what that meant. Once, when I was fasting in a jail in Colorado, she sent me a postcard with an aerial photo of Cape Cod with the message, "I hope this card refreshes you and does not tantalize you." It occurred to me that Dorothy believed that beauty itself has a moral dimension. To direct our attention to beauty, or even the recollection of it, while sitting in a slum or a jail cell or a hermitage, could inspire us to greater courage, hope, and love.

And that leads me to one last thing, which comes as a surprise to those who only know her through her dour expressions in photographs. That is how much fun it was to be with her. She had a tremendous sense of humor, and a girlish laugh.

John Cort, who joined the Catholic Worker soon after graduating from Harvard in the early 1930s, was drawn to the movement after witnessing how much fun Dorothy seemed to be having. Here was a woman who appeared to be pretty old (at the time she was in her mid-thirties) who seemed to be having the time of her life, and he wanted a share of that.

The Long Loneliness ends with a meditation in which she says "we were just sitting around talking" when everything happened—when Peter Maurin came in; when lines of people began to form; when someone said, "Let's all go and live on a farm." She says, "It was as casual as all that, I often think. It just came about. It just happened."

That is one of the things you had to experience for yourself, being around Dorothy: The unexpected things that could begin in a conversation as you just sat around talking; the way that history or your own life could suddenly take a turn as you were just sitting around the kitchen table over a cup of coffee or a bowl of soup.

It often seems that way for me, too, when I look back on my life. It just happened. And the talk, and the witness, and the daily acts of faith and love continued long after I had moved on. "You will know your vocation," Dorothy once said, "by the joy it gives you." It was not my vocation to remain serving soup at the Catholic Worker. But evidently it was my vocation to become an editor—in fact, incredibly enough, Dorothy Day's editor. And that has given me joy.

Sources

Articles by Dorothy Day from *The Catholic Worker*, whether named or drawn from her regular "On Pilgrimage" column, can be read in full online at www.CatholicWorker.org.

Other sources by Dorothy Day:

All the Way to Heaven: The Selected Letters of Dorothy Day, ed. Robert Ellsberg (Milwaukee, WI: Marquette University Press, 2010; Image Books, 2012).

Dorothy Day: Selected Writings, ed. Robert Ellsberg (Maryknoll, NY: Orbis Books, 1992).

The Duty of Delight: The Diaries of Dorothy Day, ed. Robert Ellsberg (Milwaukee, WI: Marquette University Press, 2008; Image Books, 2011).

From Union Square to Rome (New York: Preservation of the Faith Press, 1938; Maryknoll, NY: Orbis Books, 2006).

House of Hospitality (New York: Sheed and Ward, 1938; Huntington, IN: Our Sunday Visitor, 2015).

Loaves and Fishes (New York: Harper & Row, 1963; Maryknoll, NY: Orbis Books, 1997).

The Long Loneliness (New York: Harper & Row, 1952).

On Pilgrimage (Catholic Worker Books, 1948; Grand Rapids, MI: Eerdmans, 1999).

Thérèse (Springfield, IL: Templegate, 1960; Notre Dame, IN: Ave Maria Press, 2015).

INTRODUCTION

On June 15, 1955, at the sound of a wailing siren signaling an imminent nuclear attack, the entire population of New York City obediently sought shelter in basements and subway stations, or, in the case of school children, under their desks. According to the authorities, this first in a series of annual "civil defense" drills was a "complete success." Well, almost. It was marred by a middle-aged, white-haired woman and twenty-six others who refused to play along with this war game. Rather than take shelter, Dorothy Day and her companions instead sat in City Hall Park, where they were arrested and later sentenced to jail. The judge who imposed bail likened the protesters to "murderers" who had contributed to the "utter destruction of these three million theoretically killed in our city."

Of course, "three million," the number of theoretical fatalities of a nuclear strike on New York City, would hardly have measured the potential devastation. Actual plans for nuclear war involved deaths in the hundreds of millions. As Dorothy Day saw it, the illusion that nuclear war was "survivable," and therefore "winnable," made such a monstrous war more likely. To participate in such an exercise for doomsday, she believed, was an act of blasphemy. And so she went to jail.

On that clear spring day in 1955 it was more than twenty years since Dorothy Day had founded the Catholic

Worker—at first a newspaper, and then a movement consisting of "houses of hospitality" in New York City and poor neighborhoods across the country. In such communities the "works of mercy" (feeding the hungry, clothing the naked, sheltering the homeless) were combined with a commitment to social justice and the vision of a new society based on values of generosity, compassion, and solidarity, rather than selfishness, greed, and fear.

There were many who had initially admired her work among the poor. Among the original subscribers to her newspaper, founded in the heart of the Depression, there were also plenty who sympathized with her critique of an economic system that produced such poverty and desperation. Yet few, in those early years, joined Day in her conviction that the way of Jesus was incompatible with any kind of killing—a most controversial stand, which she first proclaimed during the Spanish Civil War and then maintained, even more controversially, throughout World War II. But on the day of that first civil defense drill, the number of Catholics in New York City who agreed that preparation for nuclear war was a crime against God and humanity could evidently fit inside a single police wagon. And yet for Dorothy, it all went together. The Catholic Worker was an effort to live out the radical implications of the teaching of Christ: that what we do for the least of our brothers and sisters—whether feed them, shelter them, or bomb them—we do directly for him.

* * *

It might seem curious to begin this anthology of Dorothy Day's "Spiritual Writings" with an account of civil disobedience, rather than with her discipline of prayer, her veneration of the saints, or her devotion to the sacraments. All these things and more sustained her. (When traveling, she noted, she was careful to bring her Bible, her missal, and a jar of instant coffee—all of them "essential.") Yet what caused Dorothy to stand out in her time, as it does still, is the way her spiritual life was expressed not only in her daily prayer but in her response to the needs of her neighbors, to the poor, and to the demands of history.

The case of this particular protest points to the potential stakes involved. To Dorothy, the specter of nuclear war was a modern dramatization of the biblical choice: "I call upon the heavens and the earth to witness today that I have set before you life and death, blessings and curses. Choose life, so that you and your descendants might live" (Deut 30:19). If there is a future for humanity on this planet, it may be because the spiritual option embraced by Dorothy Day has become more commonplace.

The writings collected here, however, are a reminder that the activism and public witness for which she is best remembered were merely the more visible expression of the deep spiritual synthesis that guided her daily life. Much of that centered on the practice of her traditional Catholic faith: daily Mass, the rosary, recitation of the Psalms in morning and evening prayer, observance of the feasts and fasts of the liturgical calendar. She drew inspiration from the example of favorite saints, like Francis of Assisi, St. Benedict, and Teresa of Avila (a martyrology enlarged, in her case, by favorite peacemakers, novelists, and heroes of the labor movement). But it would be hard to describe Dorothy Day simply in terms of continuity with previous models of holiness. Like the great saints she revered, she also devised her own path.

That path was marked by a number of favorite maxims that appear throughout this book: "All the way to Heaven is heaven" (St. Catherine of Siena); "The world will be saved by beauty" (Dostoevsky); "the sacrament of the present moment" (Jean-Pierre de Caussade); "the practice of the presence of God" (Brother Lawrence); "the Little Way" (St. Thérèse); "the duty of delight" (John Ruskin). Such phrases pointed to the deep significance of all the incidents, encounters, and circumstances of our daily life, when viewed in light of the gospel. Everyday life could be a school of love. Eternal life was rooted in the here and now. And the lessons mastered in small and intimate ways equipped her for larger, public challenges. Overall, she summed up her mission as a response to "the greatest challenge of the day": "How to bring about a revolution of the heart, a revolution which has to start with each one of us?"

* * *

Dorothy's revolution of the heart was rooted in two primary stories. The first of these, of course, was the Gospel story of Jesus. Along with the Eucharist, the Gospel texts were the staple of her daily life: the parables, the Sermon on the Mount, Jesus's encounters with the poor and sick, his conflicts with the religious and political authorities of his time, his passion and Resurrection. In these stories she did not encounter a figure from two thousand years ago, but a lens for reading the ordinary events of life, the news of the day, and her encounters with those in need. To be a Christian, she believed, was to live in a constant confrontation with the living Christ: "It is no use to say that we are born two thousand years too late to give room to Christ. Nor will those who live at the end of the world have been born too late. Christ is always with us, always asking for room in our hearts."

And then there was her own story, which she shared in two memoirs, *From Union Square to Rome* (1938) and *The*

Long Loneliness (1952). In both cases she was eager to relate the story of those events, encounters, and experiences in her early life that brought her to the knowledge of God. Chief among these was her engagement with the cause of the poor and the struggle for social justice. "Because I sincerely loved His poor, He taught me to know Him. And when I think of the little I ever did, I am filled with hope and love for all those others devoted to the cause of social justice."

But there were many other experiences along the way. She wrote about her childhood piety, and how, during her two years in college, this was supplanted by a new faith in the struggle for justice. She wrote about her work in New York as a journalist with left-wing newspapers and magazines, her arrest with suffragists in Washington, DC, and the dejection she experienced in her brief stints in jail. She wrote of late nights in saloons listening to Eugene O'Neill recite "The Hound of Heaven," and the impulse that often drove her, afterward, to sit at the back of St. Joseph's Church in Greenwich Village, "not knowing what was going on at the altar, but warmed and comforted by the lights and silence, the kneeling people, and the atmosphere of worship." She also referred to other experiences of "the tragic aspect of life in general," though she did not go into detail. As we now know, this included a desperate love affair that ended with her having an abortion and twice attempting to commit suicide. All this, of course, was before becoming a Catholic. Yet, from the perspective of her conversion, she came to believe that God had been present throughout this story, hovering over her life, in times of doubt and confusion as much as in joy and conviction.

In 2000 the Archdiocese of New York initiated Dorothy Day's cause for canonization, and she was named a Servant of God. Thus began a long process that may one day result in her becoming known as St. Dorothy. If so, no doubt she will be a saint with an unusual backstory. Yet even the circumstances of her conversion are unique in the annals of the saints. This occurred while she was living on Staten Island with a man she deeply loved, Forster Batterham, and discovered that she was once again pregnant. This time, in her gratitude, she welcomed the new life within her, and found herself praying and wishing to have her child baptized—a step she eventually followed in 1927, at the age of thirty.

Later, quoting a character from Dostoevsky, she would write, "All my life I have been haunted by God." And yet there was seemingly nothing inevitable about her decision to become a Catholic. She had been raised in a nominally Protestant family in which "the name of God was never mentioned," and "to speak of the soul was to speak immodestly, uncovering what might better remain hidden." Her father, a sportswriter who later described Dorothy as "the nut of the family," believed that only "Irish cops and washerwomen" were Catholics. She was baptized in the Episcopal Church at the age of twelve, but put aside any religious impulses during her two years in college. "Religion, as it was practiced by those I encountered . . . had no vitality. It had nothing to do with everyday life; it was a matter of Sunday praying. Christ no longer walked the streets of this world. He was two thousand years dead and new prophets had risen up in His place." During her time working as a writer for the *New York Call* and the *Masses*, her friends were socialists, radicals, and literary Bohemians who regarded religion as "the opiate of the people." That opinion was shared, at the time of her conversion, by Forster, her "common-law husband," as she called him. So what accounted for her attraction to Catholicism?

Throughout her life she remembered her brief encounters with certain Catholics, like the mother of a childhood friend, whose faith, despite the hardship of their circumstances, seemed to offer a sense of wholeness and transcendence. In reading William James's *Varieties of Religious Experience* she began to learn about people who inhabited a larger, spiritual world, and in the novels of Dostoevsky she was moved by stories of characters shaped by the gospel and their own experience of sin, suffering, and mercy. As she noted, "I was tired of following the devices and desires of my own heart, of doing what I wanted to do, what my desires told me I wanted to do, which always seemed to lead me astray."

She believed that the Catholic Church, for all its failures, was the church of the poor. She was attracted by its appeal to the senses: "The music speaking to the ear, the incense to the sense of smell, the appeal of color to the eye, stained glass, ikons and statues, the bread and wine to the taste, the touch of rich vestments and altar linens, the touch of holy water, oils, the sign of the cross, the beating of the breast."

And though she had passed through many times of sorrow, her conversion was ultimately born not from sadness but from the experience of what she called "natural happiness": her love for Forster, her awakening to the beauty of nature, and the joy she felt in knowing that she was going to have a baby. Her happiness made her believe in a still greater happiness. She experienced a sense of gratitude so immense that only God could receive it.

And yet her daughter's baptism, followed later by her own entry to the church, did not provide an immediate sense of arrival. For one thing, it meant separation from Forster, who, as an atheist and anarchist, refused, in principle, to get married. At the same time, in becoming a Catholic, she felt that she was betraying her comrades in the struggle for the poor and oppressed. If the church was the home of the poor, it also seemed all too often the defender of the status quo, a friend of the rich and powerful. Thus, she embarked on a lonely path for the next five years, supporting her daughter as a single mother, writing articles for the Catholic press, and pursuing work as she could find it (including a stint as a writer in Hollywood and a garden columnist on Staten Island), while searching for some higher purpose.

The turning point came in December 1932 when she traveled to Washington, DC, to write about a "hunger march" of the unemployed, organized by her former Communist friends. Why were Catholics not leading such a march, she wondered. Heading for the Shrine of the Immaculate Conception, she offered a prayer that came "with tears and with anguish" that she might find her vocation—some way of using her talents in the service of the poor. And when she returned to New York she met Peter Maurin, an itinerant French apostle in search of a collaborator, whose personalist philosophy seemed an answer to her prayer.

This realization wasn't immediately obvious, as Maurin, with his thick French accent and shabby appearance, proceeded to lecture her about history, the problems of the industrial age, the dignity of work, and the monastic ideal of hospitality. Twenty years Dorothy's senior, Maurin had been raised in a peasant family in southern France. Educated by the Christian Brothers, he had imbibed the spirit of social Catholicism before immigrating to North America, where he tramped about in poverty, engaging in hard labor, while devising a "synthesis" in the area of Catholic social philosophy. Peter Maurin believed that the troubles facing the world came from substituting the bank account for the Sermon on the Mount as the ultimate standard of values. He believed Christians should begin at once to live by gospel values, building "a new world within the shell of the old," a world "where it would be easier for people to be good."

It took a while for Dorothy to comprehend Maurin's vision and to see how it related to her own search. Yet, one of his suggestions immediately caught her attention: that she start a newspaper to promote the radical social message of the gospel. Almost immediately, she got to work. The result was the *Catholic Worker*, an eight-page tabloid composed on her kitchen table. The first issue, filled initially with stories about strikes, evictions, child labor, racial injustice, and Peter Maurin's own "Easy Essays," was launched at a May Day rally in Union Square in 1933. In her first editorial, she wrote:

> For those who are sitting on park benches in the warm spring sunlight. For those who are huddling in shelters trying to escape the rain. For those who are walking the streets in the all but futile search for work. For those who think that there is no hope for the future, no recognition of their plight—this little paper is addressed.
>
> It is printed to call their attention to the fact that the Catholic church has a social program—to let them know that there are men of God who are working not only for their spiritual but for their material welfare.

It is striking how quickly Dorothy's life had changed. Within a few months of her meeting Peter Maurin she had found not only a new work, but a new vitality and energy. It was as if her soul had been dry kindling, to which Peter Maurin applied a spark. As the editor of a newspaper and the leader of a growing movement, she was suddenly thrust onto a public stage, confidently addressing bishops, labor priests, and union leaders. She had a voice and a message— one that drew particular authority from the fact that she was living it out.

Other lay Catholics quickly answered her call and gathered to join the work. Before long, they had implemented the second plank in Maurin's program, opening a "house of hospitality," where she and her fellow "Catholic Workers" would live among the poor, in voluntary poverty, practicing the works of mercy. Before meeting Maurin, Dorothy had been searching for a "synthesis" of her own: between the spiritual and the material, this world and the next. The solution to that synthesis, she came to realize, was in the radical implications of the Incarnation. God, in Jesus, had entered our flesh and our history. All of creation, the whole material world, was thereby hallowed. We could not separate the love of God from the love of our neighbors. Jesus said that what we did for the poor, we did directly for him. In effect, this teaching became the first spiritual foundation of the Catholic Worker, expressed not only in the works of mercy, but in work for justice and peace.

* * *

Of course, by feeding a few hundred hungry people each morning she did not believe she could solve the problems of the Depression. Nor, years later, when she sat out the civil defense drills and went to jail, did she believe that such gestures would bring an end to war. But like Jesus, who spoke of the mysterious potential of a mustard seed, Dorothy believed in the power hidden in small and humble means. And this was a second, essential foundation of Dorothy's spirituality. In this she drew surprising lessons from her favorite saint, Thérèse of Lisieux.

At first glance there would appear to be little in common between these two women, Day, the activist, and Thérèse Martin, a Carmelite nun who died in 1897 (the year of Dorothy's birth) at the age of twenty-four in a small convent in Normandy.

St. Thérèse called her spiritual path the "Little Way." It consisted of performing all the small deeds and obligations of daily life in a spirit of love and in the presence of God. In this way, she believed, daily life could become an arena for holiness. You didn't have to be in a convent or face lions in the Roman Colosseum. Everyday life provided the means for sanctification. Furthermore, Thérèse believed strongly in the spiritual connections that bind all members of the Mystical Body of Christ. Thus, each sacrifice endured in love, each work of mercy, did not just advance one's own path to holiness—it might increase the balance of love in the world. As Dorothy wrote, "We can throw our pebble in the pond and be confident that its ever-widening circle will reach around the world."

Dorothy's devotion to St. Thérèse was particularly ironic in light of her original impression. Upon first reading Thérèse's autobiography, which she received from a priest soon after her conversion, she found it "colorless, monotonous, too small in fact for my notice."

> What kind of a saint was this who felt that she had to practice heroic charity in eating what was put in front of her, in taking medicine, enduring cold and heat, enduring the society of mediocre souls, in following the strict regime of the convent of Carmelite nuns which she had joined at the age of fifteen?

And yet Dorothy would come to see in Thérèse not only a great saint, but one with a particular relevance to our times.

What accounted for her change of heart? The answer lay in her experience with the Catholic Worker. Through years of living among the poor and unwanted, "eating what was put in front of her," enduring not only cold and heat but also the sights and smells of squalor and the company of many wounded souls, she came to appreciate the power of Thérèse's Little Way.

Dorothy's diaries record the discipline of her spiritual life: daily Mass, the rosary, and meditation on Scripture. But above all they show a woman who held her everyday life against the standard of the gospel—measuring and testing her own capacity for love, forgiveness, and patience. She did not have a placid disposition. "I have a hard enough job to curb the anger in my own heart which I sometimes even wake up with, go to sleep with—a giant to strive with, an ugliness, a sorrow to me—a mighty struggle to love. As long as there is any resentment, bitterness, lack of love in my own heart I am powerless. God must help me."

In her daily examination of conscience she remembered acts of kindness or incidents that reminded her of God. But she also noted failures of charity: "At 1:00 a man and woman came bringing a drunken woman in and I was very harsh in not taking her. As Tom said, before dawn came, I had denied our Lord in her. I felt very guilty—more for my manner than for doing it, as we could not have all the other women in the house disturbed." The answer was love and more love. "Thinking gloomily of the sins and shortcomings of others," she writes, "it suddenly came to me to remember my own offenses, just as heinous as those of others. If I concern myself with my own sins and lament them, if I remember my own failures and lapses, I will not be resentful of others. This was most cheering and lifted the load of gloom from my mind. It makes one unhappy to judge people and happy to love them."

The title of her diaries, *The Duty of Delight*, is taken from a phrase she often liked to repeat. It appears in the post-script to her autobiography, where she writes, "It is not easy always to be joyful, to keep in mind the duty of delight." This was another facet of Dorothy's spirituality. Anyone could feel delight when things were delightful. By the same token it was easy to love people who were lovable or who loved us in return. But the heart of the gospel, as she liked to quote St. John of the Cross, was this: "Where there is no love, put love, and you will draw love out." If we willed to love someone, if we willed to see Christ in them, we could do it. So she believed. That didn't mean it was any easier for her than for others. Yet it was the exercise of her faith in these small ways, the effort to live her daily life in the con-scious presence of God, that equipped her for the extraordi-nary actions she performed on a wider stage.

Here too, the teaching of St. Thérèse came into play. In the 1950s, at the same time as her protests of the civil defense drills, she was actually writing a book about Thérèse, moti-vated, she said, by her desire to call attention to the "social implications" of Thérèse's teachings: the significance of all the little things we do—or fail to do. This included the protests we make: appearing foolish while standing on a street corner with a sign for peace, or handing out a leaflet, or going to jail for a few days. There was no calculating the potential effect of such gestures, no matter how apparently foolish and ineffective.

In the Gospels this principle was illustrated in the story of Jesus's multiplication of the loaves and fishes. Dorothy drew on that image for the title of one of her books. In *Loaves and Fishes*, she wrote,

> One of the greatest evils of the day . . . is [the] sense
> of futility. Young people say, "What good can one
> person do? What is the sense of our small effort?"
> They cannot see that we must lay one brick at a time,
> take one step at a time; we can be responsible only
> for the action of the present moment, but we can beg
> for an increase of love in our hearts that will vitalize
> and transform all our individual actions, and know
> that God will take them and multiply them, as Jesus
> multiplied the loaves and fishes.

It may be that Dorothy's application of St. Thérèse's Little Way to the social arena is one of the most significant and at the same time underappreciated aspects of her spirituality. In a world in which everything is measured by numbers, metrics, return on investment—it is hard to appreciate that there is any other way of measuring value and success. But then how are we to understand Christ's message: that it is only if the seed falls into the ground and dies that it bears much fruit?

In a time when so many feel overwhelmed by the vast powers of this world, Dorothy Day bore witness to another power—the power disguised in what is apparently small and weak. Who can measure such power? As she noted, "We know that one impulse of grace is of infinitely more power than a cobalt bomb."

* * *

Through most of her life, Dorothy was regarded as a fairly marginal figure, far outside the mainstream of the church. As a result of her protests and work for peace she received a good deal of criticism. Some called her un-American. She was charged with being weak, irrelevant, and foolish. (In reply, she stated, "We confess to being foolish, and wish that we were more so.") She was accused of being a secret Communist. In the 1950s, J. Edgar Hoover, director of the FBI, placed her name on a list of dangerous radicals to be detained in the event of a national emergency.

And yet, by her later years the tide had definitely shifted. She was offered honorary degrees by Catholic universities, which she consistently refused. ("If you live long enough you are regarded as a venerable survivor.") In 1976 she was invited to speak, along with Mother Teresa, at the Eucharistic Congress in Philadelphia. (Her speech, reprinted in this volume, shows that she used the occasion to call for atonement for the sin of Hiroshima.) *Time* magazine included her in a special issue on "Living Saints." She was, by this time, widely regarded as the "radical conscience" of the Catholic Church in America.

Upon her death on November 29, 1980, historian David O'Brien, writing in *Commonweal*, called her "the most important, interesting, and influential figure in the history of American Catholicism." At the time this was an audacious claim. It is hard to measure the significance of a life at such close range. And yet it was amazingly prescient. Over four decades since her death, this assessment seems not only plausible, but undoubtedly true. There have obviously been many other interesting and influential American Catholics in the last two hundred years. But it would be hard to think of another American Catholic who so radically recalled the church to its gospel origins, who so prophetically anticipated the renewal of Vatican II, and who prefigured the agenda most recently outlined by Pope Francis for the universal church.

As it turned out, this judgment received some confirmation from Pope Francis himself in his address to the U.S.

xxx | Dᴏʀᴏᴛʜʏ Dᴀʏ: Sᴘɪʀɪᴛᴜᴀʟ Wʀɪᴛɪɴɢs

Congress in 2015. There, going beyond even the encomium of David O'Brien, he included Dorothy Day in the ranks of Abraham Lincoln, Martin Luther King Jr., and her friend Thomas Merton as one of the four "great Americans" around whom he organized his speech. "In these times when social concerns are so important," he said, "I cannot fail to mention the Servant of God Dorothy Day, who founded the Catholic Worker Movement. Her social activism, her passion for justice and for the cause of the oppressed were inspired by the Gospel, her faith, and the example of the saints."

In 2023 Pope Francis elaborated on his admiration for Dorothy Day in a foreword to a new edition of *From Union Square to Rome*. There he wrote that her life "exemplified what St. James said in his Letter: "Show me your faith without works and I by my works will show you my faith." The pope went on to reflect on her spirit of yearning and restlessness ("The Lord comforts restless hearts, not bourgeois souls who are content with things as they are"), her love for the church despite its evident failings, and her commitment to service, which must become political in overcoming injustice and safeguarding human dignity.

Doubtless she would have viewed all this attention with suspicion. As she often said, "Too much praise makes you feel that you must be doing something terribly wrong." In that light it is fair to wonder what she would have thought of efforts to declare her a saint.

For some, the answer is clear: "Don't call me a saint," she is famously quoted as saying. "I don't want to be dismissed that easily." Putting aside the fact that no actual saint would possibly say otherwise, there are still other reasons why this quote should not represent the last word on the subject.

No one took saints more seriously than Dorothy Day. For her, they were not idealized super-humans, but constant companions and daily guides in the imitation of Christ. She relished the human details of their struggles to be faithful, realizing full well that in their own time they were often regarded as eccentrics or dangerous troublemakers.

Yet she was aware of the tendency to put saints on a pedestal, far above the usual standard of humanity. When people referred to her as a living saint, she supposed that they imagined that things came easily for her—living with the poor, going to jail—that would be unthinkable for ordinary people. If that is what it meant to be called a saint, she would have none of it.

For Dorothy, the challenge was not to be *called* a saint but to *be* a saint. She believed this was not only her own vocation but the calling of all Christians. "We might as well get over our bourgeois fear of the name," she wrote. "We might also get used to recognizing the fact that there is some of the saint in all of us. Inasmuch as we are growing, putting off the old man and putting on Christ, there is some of the saint, the holy, the divine right there."

At the same time, however, she believed in the need for a new model of holiness in our time. This intuition came to her even as a child. Recalling her first discovery of stories about saints, she described her admiration for their heroic ministry to the poor, the weak, and the infirm. But, already, there was another question in her mind: "Why was so much done in remedying the evil instead of avoiding it in the first place? . . . *Where were the saints to try to change the social order, not just to minister to the slaves, but to do away with slavery?*" It was a question she would answer with her own life.

For Dorothy, the calling to follow Christ was not something achieved in a single moment or all at once. Recalling the conversion of St. Francis, she noted, "Sometimes it takes but one step. We would like to think so. And yet the older

I get the more I see that life is made up of many steps, and they are very small affairs, not giant strides. I have 'kissed a leper,' not once but twice—consciously—and I cannot say I am much the better for it."

The spiritual life was a journey, or a "pilgrimage," in which the significance of events and our response was determined by their relation to our final destination. The pattern of discipleship was outlined by Jesus in the Beatitudes, and it is clear that these enumerated virtues were the pattern of Dorothy's life: Blessed are the poor in spirit; the meek; the merciful; those who mourn; the pure of heart; those who hunger for God's righteousness; the peacemakers; those who are persecuted for righteousness' sake. One could write an essay on how Dorothy not only embraced each of these beatitudes but demonstrated their powerful social and counter-cultural meaning.

The relevance of Dorothy Day's life and witness is not likely to fade. Her great themes are no less urgent today: the quest for freedom, community, and peace; the sacredness of life; the dignity of the poor; the practice of mercy; the hope for "a new social order in which justice dwelleth."

To reflect on her life today, more than forty years after her death, brings to mind the words she wrote about her mentor Peter Maurin, words that could apply as well to herself. She noted that some people criticized Peter for having a holier-than-thou attitude. Well, Peter was "holier than thou," she said. "Holier than anyone we ever knew."

* * *

And what about those civil defense drills in the 1950s? Dorothy was arrested in successive annual drills and twice received sentences of thirty days. While lying in jail, during one of these experiences, a setting that might have given rise to thoughts of the futility of such a small gesture in light of the massive resources of the war machine, she instead found herself *"thinking of war and peace, and the problem of human freedom, . . . and the apathy of great masses of people who believe that nothing can be done—when I thought of these things, I was all the more confirmed in my faith in the little way of St. Thérèse. We do the minute things that come to hand, we pray our prayers, and beg also for an increase of faith—and God will do the rest."*

And perhaps her prayers were answered. In 1961 she was joined by two thousand other protesters who refused to cooperate. That turned out to be the end of the civil defense drills.

1

THE WORD MADE FLESH

Since becoming a Catholic in 1927, Dorothy sought some way to connect her faith with her commitment to the poor and oppressed. She longed, she said, "to make a synthesis reconciling body and soul, this world and the next."

The great turning point in her search came in December 1932 when she traveled to Washington, DC, to write about a Hunger March of the Unemployed, a protest organized by many of her old Communist friends. Watching this motley parade, she wondered why Catholics were not leading such a march. The next day she made her way to the Shrine of the Immaculate Conception. It was December 8, the actual feast day of this Marian devotion. There she offered up a prayer "with tears and with anguish" that "some way would open up for me to use what talents I possessed for my fellow workers, for the poor." Upon her return to New York she met Peter Maurin, who opened a path for the rest of her life.

In effect, as Dorothy came to realize, the synthesis she had been seeking was in plain sight. The doctrine of the Incarnation meant that God had entered into our humanity and our history. Jesus had united the commandment to love God and to love our neighbor, and he had identified himself directly with all who were poor, hungry, and in need: "I was hungry and you fed me; I was homeless and you sheltered me. . . . Insofar as you did these things to the least of my brothers and sisters," he explained, "you did them directly to me" (Matthew 25).

This Gospel text became a cornerstone of the Catholic Worker movement. It pointed to the establishment of houses of hospitality for the practice of the Works of Mercy. It underlay the core of Dorothy's spirituality in the effort to see Christ in our neighbor—especially in the poor: "The mystery of the poor is this: that they are Jesus and what we do for them we do directly for him." It underscored her embrace of voluntary poverty: we could not even see our neighbors in need as long as we clung to our comfort and security. But there were wider social implications. Dorothy believed it was not enough merely to feed the poor. One must also challenge a social order that consigned so many to poverty, hunger, and homelessness. To love our neighbor thus entailed a commitment to social justice. What is more, it meant working for a different world.

CHRIST IN HIS HUMANITY

A fateful prayer in Washington marked a turning point in Dorothy's life.

I watched that ragged horde and thought to myself, "These are Christ's poor. He was one of them. He was a man like other men, and He chose his friends amongst the ordinary workers. These men feel they have been betrayed by Christianity. Men are not Christian today. If they were, this sight would not be possible. Far dearer in the sight of God perhaps are these hungry ones, than all those smug, well-fed Christians who sit in their homes, cowering in fear of "the Communist menace."

I felt that these were my people, that I was part of them, I had worked for them and with them in the past, and now I was a Catholic and so could not be a Communist. I could not join this united front of protest, and I wanted to.

The feast of the Immaculate Conception was the next day, and I went out to the National Shrine and assisted at Solemn High Mass there. And the prayer that I offered up was that some way would be shown me, some way would be opened up for me to work for the poor and the oppressed.

House of Hospitality:

Upon her return from Washington, Dorothy found Peter Maurin waiting for her. Over the coming days and weeks he inspired her with a vision of a lay Catholic movement dedicated to the radical social message of the gospel. The first step would be a newspaper, The Catholic Worker, *distributed at a rally in Union Square on May 1, 1933. In introducing the paper in her first editorial, Dorothy emphasized the connection between the spiritual and material welfare of the poor, and Christ's own experience of poverty and insecurity.*

For those who are sitting on park benches in the warm spring sunlight.

For those who are huddling in shelters trying to escape the rain.

For those who are walking the streets in the all but futile search for work.

For those who think that there is no hope for the future, no recognition of their plight—this little paper is addressed.

It is printed to call their attention to the fact that the Catholic Church has a social program—to let them know that there are men of God who are working not only for their spiritual but for their material welfare. . . .

This first number of *The Catholic Worker* was planned, written, and edited in the kitchen of a tenement on Fifteenth Street, on subway platforms, on the El, the ferry. There is no editorial office, no overhead, in the way of telephone or electricity; no salaries paid. . . .

Next month someone may donate us an office. Who knows?

It is cheering to remember that Jesus Christ wandered this earth with no place to lay His head. *The foxes have holes and the birds of the air have nests, but the Son of Man has no place to lay His head.* And when we consider our fly-by-night existence, our uncertainty, we remember (with pride at sharing the honor) that the disciples supped by the seashore, and wandered through cornfields picking the ears from the stalks wherewith to make their frugal meals.

The Catholic Worker, May 1933

In her memoir, The Long Loneliness, *Dorothy elaborated on Christ's intimate familiarity with the world of the poor and the worker.*

We felt a respect for the poor and destitute as those nearest to God, as those chosen by Christ for His compassion. Christ lived among men. The great mystery of the Incarnation, which meant that God became man that man might become God, was a joy that made us want to kiss the earth in worship, because His feet once trod that same earth. It was a mystery that we as Catholics accepted, but there were also the facts of Christ's life, that He was born in a stable, that He did not come to be a temporal King, that He worked with His hands, spent the first years of His life in exile, and the rest of His early manhood in a crude carpenter shop in Nazareth. He fulfilled His religious duties in the synagogue and the temple. He trod the road in His public life and the first men He called were fishermen, small owners of boats and nets. He was familiar with the migrant worker and the proletariat, and some of His parables dealt with them. . . .

He died between two thieves because He would not be made an earthly King. He lived in an occupied country for thirty years without starting an underground movement or trying to get out from under a foreign power. His teaching transcended all the wisdom of the scribes and Pharisees, and taught us the most effective means of living in this world while preparing for the next. . . .

The Long Loneliness

It is because we forget the Humanity of Christ (present with us today in the Blessed Sacrament just as truly as when He walked with His apostles through the cornfields that Sunday long ago, breakfasting on the ears of corn) that we have ignored the material claims of our fellow man during this capitalistic, industrialist era. We have allowed our brothers and sisters, our fellow members in the Mystical Body, to be degraded, to endure slavery to a machine, to live in rat-infested holes.

This ignoring of the material body of our humanity, which Christ ennobled when He took flesh, gives rise to the aversion for religion evidenced by many workers. As a result of this worshipping of the Divinity alone of Christ and ignoring His Sacred Humanity, religious people looked to Heaven for justice, and Karl Marx could say, "Religion is the opium of the people." And Wobblies [the Industrial Workers of the World, or IWW] could say "Work and Pray— live on hay; you'll get pie in the sky when you die."

It is because we love Christ in His Humanity that we can love our brothers. It is because we see Christ in the least of God's creatures that we can talk to them of the love of God and know that what we write will reach their hearts.

June 1935

Dorothy and the Catholic Worker movement were early supporters of the liturgical movement, which promoted greater participation of the laity in worship (a reform later embraced by the Second

*Vatican Council). She believed liturgical prayer was an antidote
to individualism and a way to promote the experience of "brotherhood in the Mystical Body of Christ."*

The basis of the liturgical movement is prayer, the liturgical
prayer of the church. It is a revolt against private, individual
prayer. St. Paul said, "We know not what we should pray
for as we ought, but the Spirit Himself asketh for us with
unspeakable groanings." When we pray thus we pray *with*
Christ, not *to* Christ. When we recite prime and compline we
are using the inspired prayer of the church. When we pray
with Christ (not to Him) we realize Christ as our Brother.
We think of all men as our brothers then, as members of
the Mystical Body of Christ. "We are all members, one of
another," and, remembering this, we can never be indifferent to the social miseries and evils of the day. The dogma of
the Mystical Body has tremendous social implications.

January 1936

"I WAS HUNGRY AND YOU FED ME. . . ."

*In Matthew 25 Christ taught that our very salvation hinged on our
response to those in need. What we did to the poor we did directly
to him. Dorothy believed that this promise of salvation extended to
many who served Christ, even unknowingly, in their commitment
to the poor. She stressed this theme in her early memoir,* From
Union Square to Rome, *which was addressed to her former comrades in the radical movement.*

"I Gave Away an Onion"

Do you remember that little story that Grushenka told in
The Brothers Karamazov?

Once upon a time there was a peasant woman and a very wicked woman she was. And she died and did not leave a single good deed behind. The devils caught her and plunged her into a lake of fire. So her guardian angel stood and wondered what good deed of hers he could remember to tell God. "She once pulled up an onion in her garden," said he, "and gave it to a beggar woman." And God answered: "You take that onion then, hold it out to her in the lake, and let her take hold and be pulled out. And if you pull her out of the lake, let her come to Paradise, but if the onion breaks, then the woman must stay where she is." The angel ran to the woman and held out the onion to her. "Come," said he, "catch hold, and I'll pull you out." And he began cautiously pulling her out. He had just pulled her out, when the other sinners in the lake, seeing how she was being drawn out, began catching hold of her so as to be pulled out with her. But she was a very wicked woman and she began kicking them. "I'm to be pulled out, not you. It's my onion, not yours." As soon as she said that, the onion broke. And the woman fell into the lake and she is burning there to this day. So the angel wept and went away.

Sometimes in thinking and wondering at God's goodness to me, I have thought that it was because I gave away an onion. Because I sincerely loved His poor, He taught me to know Him. And when I think of the little I ever did, I am filled with hope and love for all those others devoted to the cause of social justice.

"What glorious hope!" [François] Mauriac writes.

There are all those who will discover that their neighbor is Jesus himself, although they belong to the mass of those who do not know Christ or who have forgotten Him. And nevertheless they will find themselves well loved. It is impossible for any one of those who has real charity in his heart not to serve Christ. Even some of those who think they hate Him, have consecrated their lives to Him; for Jesus is disguised and masked in the midst of men, hidden among the poor, among the sick, among prisoners, among strangers. Many who serve Him officially have never known who He was, and many who do not even know His name, will hear on the last day the words that open to them the gates of joy. "Those children were I, and I those working men. I wept on the hospital bed. I was that murderer in his cell whom you consoled."

But always the glimpses of God came most when I was alone. Objectors cannot say that it was fear of loneliness and solitude and pain that made me turn to Him. It was in those few years when I was alone and most happy that I found Him. I found Him at last through joy and thanksgiving, not through sorrow.

Yet how can I say that either? Better let it be said that I found Him through His poor, and in a moment of joy I turned to Him. I have said, sometimes flippantly, that the mass of bourgeois smug Christians who denied Christ in His poor made me turn to Communism, and that it was the Communists and working with them that made me turn to God.

From Union Square to Rome

A mystic may be called a man in love with God. Not one who loves God, but who is *in love with God*. And this mystical love, which is an exalted emotion, leads one to love the things of Christ. His footsteps are sacred. The steps of His passion and death are retraced down through the ages. Almost every time you step into a Church you see people making the Stations of the Cross. They meditate on the mysteries of His life, death, and resurrection, and by this they are retracing with love those early scenes and identifying themselves with the actors in those scenes.

When we suffer, we are told we suffer with Christ. We are "completing the sufferings of Christ." We suffer His loneliness and fear in the garden when His friends slept. We are bowed down with Him under the weight of not only our own sins but the sins of each other, of the whole world. We are those who are sinned against and those who are sinning. We are identified with Him, one with Him. We are members of His Mystical Body.

Often there is a mystical element in the love of a radical worker for his brother, for his fellow worker. It extends to the scene of his sufferings, and those spots where he has suffered and died are hallowed. The names of places like Everett, Ludlow, Bisbee, South Chicago, Imperial Valley, Elaine, Arkansas, and all those other places where workers have suffered and died for their cause have become sacred to the worker. You know this feeling as does every other radical in the country. Through ignorance, perhaps, you do not acknowledge Christ's name, yet, I believe you are trying to love Christ in His poor, in His persecuted ones. Whenever men have laid down their lives for their fellows, they are doing it in a measure for Him. This I still firmly believe, even though you and others may not realize it.

"Inasmuch as ye have done it unto one of the least of these brethren, you have done it unto me." Feeling this as strongly as I did, is it any wonder that I was led finally to the feet of Christ?

From Union Square to Rome

My criticism of Christians in the past, and it *still* holds good of too many of them, is that they in fact deny God and reject Him. "Amen I say to you, as long as you did it to one of these my least brethren, you did it to me" (Matt. 25:40), Christ said, and today there are Christians who affront Christ in the Negro, in the poor Mexican, the Italian, yes and the Jew. Catholics believe that man is the temple of the Holy Ghost, that he is made to the image and likeness of God. We believe that of Jew and Gentile. We believe that all men are members or potential members of the Mystical Body of Christ and since there is no time with God, we must so consider each man whether he is atheist, Jew, or Christian.

You ask do we really believe it, when we see our fellows herded like brutes in municipal lodging houses, tramping the streets and roads hungry, working at starvation wages or under an inhuman speed-up, living in filthy degrading conditions. Seeing many Christians denying Him, hating Him in the poor, is it any wonder a heresy has sprung up denying Him in word and deed?

The first commandment is that we should love the Lord our God. We can only show our love for God by our love for our fellows. "If any man say, I love God, and hateth his brother he is a liar. For he that loveth not his brother, whom he seeth, how can he love God, whom he seeth not?" (1 John 4:20).

From Union Square to Rome

CHRIST IN THE POOR

Look On the Face of Thy Christ

The long line of men begins every morning at five thirty. I can hear them coughing and talking under my window as I wake up, and see the reflection of the flames cast on the walls of my room from the fire they build in the gutter to keep warm. Many of the men bring boxes and bits of wood to cast on it, and as the line moves up, the men get a chance to warm themselves. Many of the men have no overcoats or sweaters. It is good to see that fire as I go down to Transfiguration Church to Mass. The flames are brilliant against the dark street and the sky is purple in contrast. There is never so much color during the day.

We are using now fifty large loaves or 150 small loaves of bread a day, twenty pounds of sugar, twenty cans of evaporated milk, and about seventy-five gallons of coffee. The coffee line has been going for a year this month, from six thirty to nine o'clock every morning. The staff takes turns at getting up to serve the line and it takes three to run it.

I write these lines because it is you, our readers, I am asking for help. Our Lord said that when you have a feast, do not invite your friends and neighbors who have plenty, but go out and bring in the destitute. If you cannot feed the hungry yourselves, give us the aid that will help us to do it for you. Our Lord will love you for it, for after all, we must remember that each of these seven hundred men or so represents Christ to us. The dignity they still possess is theirs because Christ by sharing our human nature has dignified and ennobled it.

I do not believe for one minute that we will have to stop our line. How can we lack faith when we can say each morning after Mass, "Look on the face of Thy Christ"— Christ presents us with His humanity and Divinity at that moment, and is present in the least of His children?

December 1937

Letter to the Unemployed

It is hard to preach the Gospel to men with empty stomachs, Abbé Lugan said. We are not a mission. We turn off the melancholy religious offerings on the radio in the morning. Religion is joy in the Holy Spirit. "Religion is a fire; it is like the coming of the Paraclete, 'a mighty wind rising'; it is a passion, the most powerful passion known to man. For religion is 'mighty to God unto the pulling down of fortifications.' Religion is a battle," writes Father Gillis.

Because it is a battle, and because you are not weaklings, we fight our own inclinations to feed only bodies to the small extent we can and let this editorial go. But it is a battle to hang on to religion when discouragement sets in. It is a battle to remember that we are made in the image and likeness of God when employers, treating you with less consideration than animals, turn you indifferently away. It is a fierce battle to maintain one's pride and dignity, to remember that we are brothers of Christ, who ennobled our human nature by sharing it.

But that very thought should give courage and should bring hope.

Christ was a worker and in the three years He roamed through Palestine He had no place to lay His head. But He said, "Take no thought for what ye shall eat and where ye shall sleep, or what ye shall put on. Seek ye first the Kingdom of God and His righteousness and all these things shall be added unto you. . . . For your Heavenly Father knoweth that you have need of these things."

For one year now, our coffee line has been going on. Right now we are making seventy-five gallons of coffee every morning. There are too many of you for us, who wait on the line, to talk to you. We must think of the other fellow waiting out in the cold, as you remember, for you are very prompt in finishing your breakfast and making way for them. It is a grim and desperate struggle to keep the line going in more ways than one.

It is hard, I repeat, to talk to you of religion. But without faith in each other, we cannot go on. Without hope we cannot go on. Without hope we cannot live. To those who are without hope, I remind you of Christ, your brother. Religion, thought in terms of our brotherhood through Christ, is not the opiate of the people. It is a battle "mighty to God unto the pulling down of fortifications." Do not let either capitalist or Communist kill this noble instinct in you.

December 1937

Last night I sat next to some of the Bowery men, living on relief in lodging houses or sleeping in doorways. They were as poor, as destitute, as down and out as a man can get. How close they are to our Lord!

Christ was a man so much like other men that it took the kiss of a Judas to single Him out, Mauriac wrote.

He was like that man in the pew beside me. He was as like him as his brother. He was His brother. And I felt Christ in that man beside me and loved him.

Every morning I break my fast with the men on the breadline. Some of them speak to me, many do not. But they know me and I know them. And there is a sense of comradeship there. We "know each other in the breaking of bread."

March 1939

You can look at all the men at all the houses and see them as pretty rotten. That, of course, is the way we should see things; to see men as but dust; from the human point of view that is perfectly true, and we should have to have a dictator with an iron hand getting them regimented and whipped into line and making them do what they should do.

But from the standpoint of the supernatural they are a little less than the angels, and if we could only keep that attitude towards them! When we are in love with people we see all the best that there is in them and understand very clearly their failures and their lapses. But the love continues strong and works wonders.

I often think that our Lord must have been terribly bored with the disciples very often, humanly speaking. Certainly he wasn't picking out brilliant, accomplished, pleasing personalities with whom to live. Isn't it in today's epistle where the mother of James and John wanted the best place for her two sons? So even the relatives were hanging on to see what they could get out of the situation. He certainly had to get away from them every now and then and do a lot of praying.

If we could only keep this early fervor and enthusiasm about people.

A friend of mine, Mrs. Livingston, was telling me about a story she read in *The Saturday Evening Post* of all places a year or so ago in which a young girl is wildly in love with a wastrel until later on when this had been broken up and she had been married for a year to a man of good solid character, she ran into her former love again.

She confessed to her husband that she had been afraid of meeting him for fear some of the old glamour remained, and she said to him: "Now I can see him as he is." And her husband, who must have been a man of great discernment, said to her very sadly: "Perhaps it was before that you were seeing him as he really is." Or as he was meant to be, which is what he wanted to bring out.

This story brings out the idea of the kind of love we ought to have for people, a love which sees their value, and sees them as God intended them to be, rather than seeing them as they are outwardly.

They say that a mystic is someone who is in love with God, again using that comparison as the kind of love we should feel. This is one of the most absorbing problems of all the work, this relationship we have to all those around us, the tie that holds us all around the country together.

I have said over and over again that Catholics have more faith in God than they have in man and that is the trouble with religion. It is a transferring of our hopes from earth to heaven and from man to God to such an extent that we turn to pie in the sky and forget that we are all members of the Mystical Body of Christ right here on this earth.

It is one of the good things about the Communist heresy that they have seen this aspect of the truth, this necessity for recognizing human dignity and the nobility and grandeur of man, man who is a little less than the angels, who has been placed "over the work of His hands with all things set under his feet." That psalm certainly paints a magnificent picture of what man is "that God should be mindful of him." And we have got to think of every man on the breadline and every man living in the house in that way.

It is a terrible struggle and it will go on all through our lives and perhaps we won't see any fruit of this vision, any materialization of this vision, let us say, immediately around us. Everybody is going to condemn us for wasting our time on drunks and bums and people who don't respond in any way to these ideas.

Letter to the Buffalo
Catholic Worker, [undated] 1940,
All the Way to Heaven

The Holy Family

For each family that is with us, and each family we come in contact with, let us pray, keeping in mind the Holy Family which dwelt in peace and poverty and love and joy. Sometimes it is hard to see Christ in his poor. Sometimes it is hard to see the Blessed Mother in women we come in contact with. But if we minister to each other, as we would want to serve the Holy Family, not judging the faults of others, but serving them with joy and with respect, then that is the true way of seeing Christ in our neighbor. If He thought them worth dying for, who are we to judge?

I remember one family on the west side, a longshoreman who got only a day or so on the docks every few weeks. He drank, his wife drank, and their children were growing up disorderly and dishonest. No one would help them. They sold the clothes they were given for liquor. The relief people said the man had work and didn't report it to them. Consequently often the family went hungry. We spent all one winter giving food and clothing to this family. It was indeed hard to see Christ in these poor. Yet for no other reason could we help them. Without the religious motive, it was a waste of time. With this motive, not one crumb of our help was wasted. Provided we did it with love. And of course if you help people, you soon begin to love them. Just as gratitude makes you love people.

January 2, 1940, *The Duty of Delight*

CHRIST IN DISGUISE

The love of the humanity of our Lord is the love of our brother. The only way we have to show our love for God is by the love we have for our brother. "Inasmuch as you have done it unto one of the least of these My brethren, you have done it unto Me." "You love God as much as the one you love the least."

Love of brother means voluntary poverty, stripping one's self, putting off the old man, denying one's self, etc. It also means non-participation in those comforts and luxuries which have been manufactured by the exploitation of others. While our brothers suffer, we must compassionate them, suffer with them. While our brothers suffer from lack of necessities, we will refuse to enjoy comforts. These resolutions, no matter how hard they are to live up to, no matter

how often we fall and have to begin over again, are part of
the vision and the long-range view which Peter Maurin has
been trying to give us these past ten years.

December 1944

Room for Christ

It is no use to say that we are born two thousand years too
late to give room to Christ. Nor will those who live at the
end of the world have been born too late. Christ is always
with us, always asking for room in our hearts.

But now it is with the voice of our contemporaries that
He speaks, with the eyes of store clerks, factory workers,
and children that He gazes; with the hands of office workers, slum dwellers, and suburban housewives that He gives.
It is with the feet of soldiers and tramps that He walks, and
with the heart of anyone in need that He longs for shelter.
And giving shelter or food to anyone who asks for it, or
needs it, is giving it to Christ.

We can do now what those who knew Him in the days
of His flesh did. I'm sure that the shepherds did not adore
and then go away to leave Mary and her Child in the stable,
but somehow found them room, even though what they
had to offer might have been primitive enough. All that
the friends of Christ did for Him in His lifetime we can do.
Peter's mother-in-law hastened to cook a meal for Him, and
if anything in the Gospels can be inferred, it is surely that
she gave the very best she had, with no thought of extrava-
gance. Matthew made a feast for Him and invited the whole
town, so that the house was in an uproar of enjoyment, and
the straight-laced Pharisees—the good people—were scan-
dalized.

The people of Samaria, despised and isolated, were over-
joyed to give Him hospitality, and for days He walked and
ate and slept among them. And the loveliest of all relation-

ships in Christ's life, after His relationship with his Mother, is His friendship with Martha, Mary, and Lazarus and the continual hospitality He found with them. It is a staggering thought that there were once two sisters and a brother whom Jesus looked on almost as His family and where He found a second home, where Martha got on with her work, bustling round in her house-proud way, and Mary simply sat in silence with Him.

If we hadn't got Christ's own words for it, it would seem raving lunacy to believe that if I offer a bed and food and hospitality for some man, woman, or child, I am replaying the part of Lazarus or Martha or Mary and that my guest is Christ. There is nothing to show it, perhaps. There are no haloes already glowing round their heads—at least none that human eyes can see. It is not likely that I shall be vouchsafed the vision of Elizabeth of Hungary, who put the leper in her bed and later, going to tend him, saw no longer the leper's stricken face, but the face of Christ. The part of a Peter Claver, who gave a stricken Negro his bed and slept on the floor at his side, is more likely to be ours. For Peter Claver never saw anything with his bodily eyes except the exhausted black faces of the Negroes; He had only faith in Christ's own words that these people were Christ. And when on one occasion the Negroes he had induced to help him ran from the room, panic-stricken before the disgusting sight of some sickness, he was astonished. "You mustn't go," he said, and you can still hear his surprise that anyone could forget such a truth; "You mustn't leave him—it is Christ."

Some time ago I saw the death notice of a sergeant-pilot who had been killed on active service. After the usual information, a message was added which, I imagine, is likely to be imitated. It said that anyone who had ever known the dead boy would always be sure of a welcome at his parents' home. So, even now that the war is over, the father and mother will go on taking in strangers for the simple reason that they will be reminded of their dead son by the friends he made.

That is rather like the custom that existed among the first generations of Christians, when faith was a bright fire that warmed more than those who kept it burning. In every house then a room was kept ready for any stranger who might ask for shelter; it was even called "the strangers' room"; and this not because these people, like the parents of the dead airman, thought they could trace something of someone they loved in the stranger who used it, not because the man or woman to whom they gave shelter reminded them of Christ, but because—plain and simple and stupendous fact—he was Christ.

It would be foolish to pretend that it is easy always to remember this. If everyone were holy and handsome, with "alter Christus" shining in neon lighting from them, it would be easy to see Christ in everyone. If Mary had appeared in Bethlehem clothed, as St. John says, with the sun, a crown of twelve stars on her head, and the moon under her feet, then people would have fought to make room for her. But that was not God's way for her nor is it Christ's way for Himself, now when He is disguised under every type of humanity that treads the earth.

To see how far one realizes this, it is a good thing to ask honestly what you would do, or have done, when a beggar asked at your house for food. Would you—or did you—give it on an old cracked plate, thinking that was good enough? Do you think that Martha and Mary thought that the old and chipped dish was good for their guest?

In Christ's human life there were always a few who made up for the neglect of the crowd. The shepherds did it; their hurrying to the crib atoned for the people who would flee from Christ. The wise men did it; their journey across the world made up for those who refused to stir one hand's breadth from the routine of their lives to go to Christ. Even the gifts that the wise men brought have in themselves an obscure recompense and atonement for what would follow later in this Child's life. For they brought gold, the king's emblem, to make up for the crown of thorns that He would wear; they offered incense, the symbol of praise, to make up for the mockery and the spitting; they gave Him myrrh, to heal and soothe, and He was wounded from head to foot and no one bathed his wounds. The women at the foot of the cross did it too, making up for the crowd who stood by and sneered.

We can do it too, exactly as they did. We are not born too late. We do it by seeing Christ and serving Christ in friends and strangers, in everyone we come in contact with.

All this can be proved, if proof is needed, by the doctrines of the Church. We can talk about Christ's Mystical Body, about the vine and the branches, about the Communion of Saints. But Christ Himself has proved it for us, and no one has to go further than that. For He said that a glass of water given to a beggar was given to Him. He made heaven hinge on the way we act towards Him in his disguise of commonplace, frail, and ordinary human beings.

Did you give me food when I was hungry?

Did you give me something to drink when I was thirsty?

Did you take me in when I was homeless and a stranger?

Did you give me clothes when my own were all rags?

Did you come to see me when I was sick or in prison or in trouble?

And to those who say, aghast, that they never had a chance to do such a thing, that they lived two thousand years too late, He will say again what they had the chance of knowing all their lives, that if these things were done for the very least of his brethren they were done for Him.

For a total Christian the goad of duty is not needed—always prodding him to perform this or that good deed. It is not a duty to help Christ, it is a privilege. Is it likely that Martha and Mary sat back and considered that they had done all that was expected of them—is it likely that Peter's mother-in-law grudgingly served the chicken she had meant to keep till Sunday because she thought it was "her duty"? She did it gladly: she would have served ten chickens if she had them.

If that is the way they gave hospitality to Christ it is certain that is the way it should still be given. Not for the sake of humanity. Not because it might be Christ who stays with us, comes to see us, takes up our time. Not because these people remind us of Christ, as those soldiers and airmen remind the parents of their son, but because they *are* Christ, asking us to find room for Him exactly as He did at the first Christmas.

December 1945

Charity Grown Cold

Charity has grown cold, because the priest is removed in his fine rectory from the people. It is not necessary to cite instances. They can be multiplied by the thousand. The young priest soon becomes embittered and tells stories about how he is taken in. There was a terrible letter about beggars in *America*, the Jesuit weekly, last winter, complaining of their dishonesty. A Franciscan wrote it. There was a masterpiece of a letter in answer from John Cogley, one of the editors of *Today*, in Chicago, who pointed out that the poor were poor in everything these days, in honor, in virtue, in all attractiveness. It is indeed hard to see Christ in the undeserving poor, in His most degraded guise. We admit that there will always be the poor, the wastrel, the drunk, the sinner. But Christ came to save them. He loved them.

We just insist that there do not need to be so many of them, the degraded, the twisted, the warped, the miserable ones, employed and unemployed.

March 1947

The Mystery of the Poor

On Holy Thursday, truly a joyful day, I was sitting at the supper table at St. Joseph's House on Chrystie Street and looking around at all the fellow workers and thinking how hopeless it was for us to try to keep up appearances. . . .

I looked around and the general appearance of the place was, as usual, home-like, informal, noisy, and comfortably warm on a cold evening. And yet, looked at with the eyes of a visitor, our place must look dingy indeed, filled as it always is with men and women, some children too, all of whom bear the unmistakable mark of misery and destitution. Aren't we deceiving ourselves, I am sure many of them think, in the works we are doing? What are we accomplishing for them anyway, or for the world or for the common good?

"Are these people being rehabilitated?" is the question we get almost daily from visitors or from our readers (who seem to be great letter writers). One priest had his catechism classes write us questions as to our work after they had the assignment in religion class to read my book *The Long Loneliness*. The majority of them asked the same question: "How can you see Christ in people?" And we only say: It is an act of faith, constantly repeated. It is an act of love, resulting from an act of faith. It is an act of hope, that we can awaken these same acts in their hearts, too, with the help of God, and the Works of Mercy, which you, our readers, help us to do, day in and day out over the years.

On Easter Day, on awakening late after the long midnight services in our parish church, I read over the last chapter of the four Gospels and felt that I had received great light and understanding with the reading of them. "They have taken the Lord out of His tomb and we do not know where they have laid Him," Mary Magdalene said, and we can say this with her in times of doubt and questioning. How do we know we believe? How do we know we indeed have faith? Because we have seen His hands and His feet in the poor around us. He has shown Himself to us in them. We start by loving them for Him, and we soon love them for themselves, each one a unique person, most special!

In that last glorious chapter of St. Luke, Jesus told His followers, "Why are you so perturbed? Why do questions arise in your minds? Look at My hands and My feet. It is I Myself. Touch Me and see. No ghost has flesh and bones as you can see I have." They were still unconvinced, for it seemed too good to be true. "So He asked them, 'Have you anything to eat?' They offered Him a piece of fish they had cooked which He took and ate before their eyes."

How can I help but think of these things every time I sit down at Chrystie Street or Peter Maurin Farm and look around at the tables filled with the unutterably poor who are going through their long-continuing crucifixion. It is most surely an exercise of faith for us to see Christ in each other. But it is through such exercise that we grow and the joy of our vocation assures us we are on the right path.

Most certainly, it is easier to believe now that the sun warms us, and we know that buds will appear on the sycamore trees in the wasteland across from the Catholic Worker office, that life will spring out of the dull clods of that littered park across the way. There are wars and rumors of war, poverty and plague, hunger and pain. Still, the sap is rising, again there is the resurrection of spring, God's continuing promise to us that He is with us always, with His comfort and joy, if we will only ask.

The mystery of the poor is this: That they are Jesus, and what you do for them you do for Him. It is the only way we have of knowing and believing in our love. The mystery of poverty is that by sharing in it, making ourselves poor in giving to others, we increase our knowledge of and belief in love.

April 1964

2

THE LIFE OF FAITH

Following in the tradition of St. Augustine, St. Thérèse, and many others, Dorothy Day saw her life as a kind of spiritual text—a living gospel—in which God's story could be read. She shared that story in two accounts of her conversion, first in From Union Square to Rome *(1938) and later in* The Long Loneliness *(1952). In both accounts she reviewed her early life from the perspective of her conversion, tracing the events and encounters that prepared the way. These included certain intimations of faith, especially through the example of Catholics she met along the way, and the mysteries of nature; experiences of sadness and dejection that made her feel there must be more to life; her engagement with social radicals and their commitment to the cause of the poor and oppressed; and, in a special way, the experience of joy and love she felt following the birth of her daughter. Altogether, she believed, it was a story of grace.*

Yet, for Dorothy, her conversion marked only the beginning of the life of faith. This theme was especially emphasized in the retreats, which became a regular feature of Catholic Worker life in the 1940s. Led in particular by Fr. John Hugo and Fr. Pacifique Roy, they stressed the ongoing need to grow in faith and the ongoing call to conversion and holiness.

A SPIRITUAL JOURNEY

I remember the first radio I had in the early 20s, constructed for me by Willy Green, a 12-year-old, out of a cigar box, a crystal and a bit of wire, an aerial and earphones. Manipulated properly, from my seashore bungalow in Staten Island, I could hear a presidential campaign, Saturday p.m. broadcasts, football, and miracle of miracles, symphonic music. That little radio was a miracle box. I could not understand it. If *this* is possible, anything is. Planting a garden, reaping a harvest. . . . Having a baby, the greatest miracle of all.

So I could take on faith the truths of Christianity, the Church, the sacraments. My heart swelled with gratitude.

Faith came to me just like that and the need to adore.

I could not understand the mechanism of that little box with its crystal, set like a jewel to be touched by a bit of wire. It was a miracle to hear voices of people in conversation, a symphony orchestra playing Beethoven.

If I could not understand scientific truths, why should I worry about understanding spiritual truths of religion? I wanted to say yes, this is true.

February 15, 1977, *The Duty of Delight*

Whenever I felt the beauty of the world in song or story, in the material universe around me, or glimpsed it in human love, I wanted to cry out with joy. The Psalms were an outlet for this enthusiasm of joy or grief—and I suppose my writing was also an outlet. After all, one must communicate ideas. I always felt the common unity of our humanity; the longing of the human heart is for this communion. If only I could sing, I thought, I would shout before the Lord, and call upon the world to shout with me, "All ye works of the Lord, bless ye the Lord, praise Him and glorify Him forever." My idea of heaven became one of fields and meadows, sweet with flowers and songs and melodies unutterable, in which even the laughing gull and the waves on the shore would play their part.

The Long Loneliness

A childhood memory from Dorothy's early life in Chicago.

Mrs. Barrett

It was Mrs. Barrett who gave me my first impulse toward Catholicism. It was around ten o'clock in the morning that I went up to Kathryn's to call for her to come out and play. There was no one on the porch or in the kitchen. The breakfast dishes had all been washed. They were long railroad apartments, those flats, and thinking the children must be in the front room, I burst in and ran through the bedrooms.

In the front bedroom Mrs. Barrett was on her knees, saying her prayers. She turned to tell me that Kathryn and the children had all gone to the store and went on with her praying. And I felt a warm burst of love toward Mrs. Barrett that I have never forgotten, a feeling of gratitude and happiness that still warms my heart when I remember her. She had God, and there was beauty and joy in her life.

All through my life what she was doing remained with me. And though I became oppressed with the problem of poverty and injustice, though I groaned at the hideous sordidness of man's lot, though there were years when I clung to the philosophy of economic determinism as an explanation of man's fate, still there were moments when in the midst of misery and class strife, life was shot through with glory. Mrs. Barrett in her sordid little tenement flat finished her breakfast dishes at ten o'clock in the morning and got down on her knees and prayed to God.

From Union Square to Rome

Despite these early glimmers of faith, Dorothy turned from religion when she went to college. "Religion as it was practiced by those I encountered (and the majority were indifferent) had no vitality. It had nothing to do with everyday life; it was a matter of Sunday praying. Christ no longer walked the streets of this world. He was two thousand years dead and new prophets had risen up in his place." As she noted, "I was in love with the masses."

In New York, during the bitterly cold winter of 1917–18, Dorothy was working on a radical journal, The Liberator, *while spending many evenings in Greenwich Village with playwright Eugene O'Neill and other writers. "No one ever wanted to go to bed, no one ever wanted to be alone."*

It was on one of these cold, bitter winter evenings that I first heard *The Hound of Heaven,* that magnificent poem of Francis Thompson. Gene could recite all of it, and he used to sit there, looking dour and black, his head sunk on his chest, sighing, "And now my heart is as a broken fount wherein tear-drippings stagnate." It is one of those poems that awakens the soul, recalls to it the fact that God is its destiny. The idea of this pursuit fascinated me, the inevitableness of it, the recurrence of it, made me feel that inevitably I would have to pause in the mad rush of living to remember my first beginning and last end.

You will be surprised but there was many a morning after sitting all night in taverns or coming from balls over at Webster Hall that I went to an early Mass at St. Joseph's Church on Sixth Avenue. It was just around the corner from where I lived, and seeing people going to an early weekday Mass attracted me. What were they finding there? I seemed to feel the faith of those about me and I longed for their faith. My own life was sordid and yet I had had occasional glimpses of the true and the beautiful. So I used to go in and kneel in a back pew of St. Joseph's, and perhaps I asked even then, "God, be merciful to me, a sinner."

From Union Square to Rome

In 1925 Dorothy was living on Staten Island with the man she loved, Forster Batterham, and discovered that she was going to have a baby. "For a long time I thought I could not have a child," she wrote. She had been "passing through some years of fret and strife, beauty and ugliness, and even weeks of sadness and despair," but now she felt a "quiet beauty and happiness." She found herself beginning to pray.

I was thinking the other day of how inadequately we pray. Often in saying the Our Father, I find myself saying by rote the first four lines and throwing my heart into the last, asking for bread and grace and forgiveness. This selfishness humiliates me so that I go back to the beginning again in order to give thanks. "Hallowed be Thy Name. Thy kingdom come." Often I say no other prayer.

I am surprised that I am beginning to pray daily. I began because I had to. I just found myself praying. I can't get down on my knees, but I can pray while I am walking. If I get down on my knees I think, "Do I really believe? Whom am I praying to?" And a terrible doubt comes over me, and a sense of shame, and I wonder if I am praying because I am lonely, because I am unhappy.

But when I am walking up to the village for the mail, I find myself praying again, holding the rosary in my pocket that Mary Gordon gave me in New Orleans two years ago. Maybe I don't say it right but I keep saying it because it makes me happy.

Then I think suddenly, scornfully, "Here you are in a stupor of content. You are biological. Like a cow. Prayer with you is like the opiate of the people." And over and over again in my mind that phrase is repeated jeeringly, "Religion is the opiate of the people."

"But," I reason with myself, "I am praying because I am happy, not because I am unhappy. I did not turn to God in unhappiness, in grief, in despair—to get consolation, to get something from Him."

And encouraged that I am praying because I want to thank Him, I go on praying. No matter how dull the day, how long the walk seems, if I feel low at the beginning of the walk, the words I have been saying have insinuated themselves into my heart before I have done, so that on the trip back I neither pray nor think but am filled with exultation.

Along the beach I find it appropriate to say the *Te Deum* which I learned in the Episcopalian church. When I am working about the house, I find myself addressing the Blessed Virgin and turning toward her statue.

It is so hard to say how this delight in prayer has been growing on me. Two years ago, I was saying as I planted seeds in the garden, "I must believe in these seeds, that they fall into the earth and grow into flowers and radishes and beans. It is a miracle to me because I do not understand it. Neither do naturalists understand it. The very fact that they use glib technical phrases does not make it any the less a miracle, and a miracle we all accept. Then why not accept God's miracles?"

I am going to Mass now regularly on Sunday mornings. . . .

From Union Square to Rome

The birth of Tamar Teresa in March 1926 was a source of great joy. But Dorothy's happiness was divided. She had decided she would have her child baptized. Yet Forster, a committed atheist and anarchist, had no use for religion, and did not believe in marriage. She sensed that her growing impulse toward faith would lead to division.

My child was born in March at the end of a harsh winter. In December I had to come in from the country and take a little apartment in town. It was good to be there, close to friends, close to a church where I could stop and pray. I read the *Imitation of Christ* a great deal. I knew that I was going to have my child baptized a Catholic, cost what it may. I knew that I was not going to have her floundering through many years as I had done, doubting and hesitating, undisciplined and amoral. I felt it was the greatest thing I could do for a child. For myself, I prayed for the gift of faith. I was sure, yet not sure. I postponed the day of decision.

A woman does not want to be alone at such a time. Even the most hardened, the most irreverent, is awed by the stupendous fact of creation. No matter how cynically or casually the worldly may treat the birth of a child, it remains spiritually and physically a tremendous event. God pity the woman who does not feel the fear, the awe, and the joy of bringing a child into the world.

Becoming a Catholic would mean facing life alone, and I clung to family life. It was hard to contemplate giving up a mate in order that my child and I could become members of the Church. [Forster] would have nothing to do with religion or with me if I embraced it. So I waited. . . .

These pages are hard to write. The struggle was too personal. It was exceedingly difficult. The year passed and it was not until the following winter that the tension reached the breaking point. My health was bad, but a thorough examination at the Cornell clinic showed only nervous strain.

Finally with precipitation, with doubts on my part at my own unseemly haste, I made the resolution to bring an end to my hesitation and be baptized.

It was in December, 1927, a most miserable day, and the trip was long from the city down to Tottenvile, Staten Island. All the way on the ferry through the foggy bay I felt grimly that I was being too precipitate. I had no sense of peace, no joy, no conviction even that what I was doing was right. It was just something that I had to do, a task to be gotten through. I doubted myself when I allowed myself to think. I hated myself for being weak and vacillating. A most consuming restlessness was upon me so that I walked around and around the deck of the ferry, almost groaning in anguish of spirit. Perhaps the devil was on the boat.

Sister Aloysia was there waiting for me, to be my godmother. I do not know whether I had any other godparent. Father Hyland, gently, with reserve, with matter-of-factness, heard my confession and baptized me.

I was a Catholic at last though at that moment I never felt less the joy and peace and consolation which I know from my own later experiences religion can bring.

A year later my confirmation was indeed joyful and Pentecost never passes without a renewed sense of happiness and thanksgiving. It was only then that the feeling of uncertainty finally left me, never again to return, praise God!

From Union Square to Rome

The ceremony of baptism is certainly impressive, with the priest beginning, "What dost thou ask of the Church of God" and the sponsor answering for the child, "Faith."

It made me think of my days of struggle coming into the Church, how I did not know whether or not I had faith or believed, or just wanted to believe. Things that I questioned I just put out of my mind then, and reconciled myself with the thought, after all, why should I expect to understand everything—that would be heaven indeed. I knew that if I waited to understand, if I waited to get rid of all my doubts, I would never be ready. So I went in all haste one December day right after Christmas, and was baptized a Catholic. I did not think of it at the time, I understood so little, that when I went to be baptized I asked for faith. But I knew that prayer, "Lord, I believe, help Thou mine unbelief," and that comforted me. Fr. Roy used to teach us to pray, "Lord, I love you because I want to love you." And recently, I read in [Réginald] Garrigou-LaGrange the quotation, from Pascal, "Thou wouldst not seek Him if Thou hadst not already found Him." So much has to be accepted by faith, and faith is so much an act of the will. And though we are informed by our senses, we hear with our ears, we read with our eyes, we understand with the interior senses; still when it comes down to it, we cannot look for sensible consolations from our faith (except very seldom). People often talk about not going to Church because they do not "feel" like going. They only pray when they "feel" like it, and when they force themselves they seem hypocritical to themselves. I used to get down on my knees with such hesitation, thinking self-consciously, "What kind of a gesture is this I am making? What am I doing this for anyway? Am I trying to induce an emotion of religion?" It is true that I was performing an act of religion, and by going through the gestures I would be more likely to "feel" reverent, adoring.

March 1948, *On Pilgrimage*

No Time with God

St. Teresa said she so loved to hear the word of God preached that she could listen with enjoyment to the poorest preacher. I know what she meant. Just as long as it is the word of God, and not politics, finances, and labor discussions from the altar. . . .

I have a very bad habit of conversing with the preacher in my mind as I listen to him and sometimes contradicting him. Tonight for instance, he told a story of sudden death to a person in mortal sin, and the hopelessness of the loved one left behind. And I remembered suddenly a young boy I knew who had committed suicide. I had asked a priest afterward as to praying for a suicide, and he said, *"There is no time with God,* and perhaps He foresees the prayers you will say and so gave him time to turn to Him at that last moment with love and longing and repentance."

That has comforted me much in thinking of old friends and associates in the radical movement who have died, who have been put to death, who have committed suicide. It makes me pray daily for Sacco and Vanzetti, for Alexander Berkman, for others who died as far as we know, estranged from God.

I thought that night as I listened, "The mothers in this congregation know that hope in the mercy of God. Some of them perhaps have sons who have met sudden violent death. There have been two murders that we know of on this street in the past year. And there was that longshoreman who was crushed to death last month by a ton of falling iron. There was our old janitor who died of gas poisoning last week. Their mothers and their loved ones know that God will hear their prayers. He knows we must bear one another's burdens. This strong hope, this boundless faith no loving God can withstand."

March 1939

A Conversation about Faith

This month I think of my mother, who died a few years ago on the feast of St. Raphael, the patron of travelers.

"My soul hath thirsted after the strong living God; when shall I come and appear before the face of God?"

But the psalmist also says, "In death there is no one that is mindful of thee." So it made me happy that I could be with my mother the last few weeks of her life, and for the last ten days at her bedside daily and hourly. Sometimes I thought to myself that it was like being present at a birth to sit by a dying person and see their intentness on what is happening to them. It almost seems that one is absorbed in a struggle, a fearful, grim, physical struggle, to breathe, to swallow, to live. And so, I kept thinking to myself, how necessary it is for one of their loved ones to be beside them, to pray for them, to offer up prayers for them unceasingly, as well as to do all those little offices one can.

When my daughter was a little tiny girl, she said to me once, "When I get to be a great big woman and you are a little tiny girl, I'll take care of you," and I thought of that when I had to feed my mother by the spoonful and urge her to eat her custard. How good God was to me, to let me be there. I had prayed so constantly that I would be beside her when she died; for years I had offered up that prayer. And God granted it quite literally. I was there, holding her hand, and she just turned her head and sighed. That was her last breath, that little sigh; and her hand was warm in mine for a long time after.

It was hard to talk about dying, but every now and then we did. But I told her that we could no more imagine the life beyond the grave than a blind man could imagine colors. We talked about faith, and how we could go just so far in our reasoned belief, and that our knowledge was like a bridge which came to an end, so that it did not reach the other shore. A wonderful prayer, that one. "I believe, O God. Help Thou mine unbelief."

The beautiful flowers around her bedside were like a gorgeous promise of the new life to come. In winter everything seems so dead—the ground, the trees, and all the shrubbery around the house—and then in a few short months things begin to stir, palpably, and life bursts forth again. Mother had seen seventy-five autumns. Seventy-five times had she seen those promises fulfilled.

Life is changed, not taken away. . .

November 1948, *On Pilgrimage*

ALL IS GRACE

For some years Dorothy planned to write a book called All Is Grace, *an account of the Retreat movement and the priests and spiritual advisors who had played a role in her life. She never finished it. The title was drawn from a line by St. Thérèse of Lisieux, echoed by the dying priest in the novel by Georges Bernanos,* Diary of a Country Priest.

"All Is Grace."

How shall I explain the title of this book? What is grace? A catechism definition is, "participation in the divine life." A Quaker would say, "that which is of God in every man."

A popular slogan to attach to a car right now is "I am loved," but what really indicates grace is "I love." Something like being in love has entered my life to transform it. It is a sense of well-being; "all is well, all will be very well," Julian of Norwich writes. To paraphrase her further: "The worst has already happened (the Fall) and it has been repaired" (Christ's death and resurrection from the dead). There is nothing now to worry about. All is grace. All things work together for those who love God.

Grace is free. If you clutch at it, it is gone. Grace is faith. "Tho He slay me, yet will I trust in Him."

Life of grace is life in that other dimension where like God we gaze upon Creation, human and earth and all that they contain and see that they are good. But who is good? Only one is good, God alone. To turn from Him willingly is to turn to chaos, even to an exultation in chaos and destruction, to emptiness and despair.

"What have I on earth but Thee, O Lord, and what do I desire in Heaven besides Thee? Hope thou in God. He is the health of thy countenance, the joy of thy youth." If one is in love, it is to see beauty everywhere, in every face. "I know not ugliness. It is a mood which has forsaken me," Max Bodenheim wrote once, or did he just declaim it as he wandered in and out of taverns in Greenwich Village? "The world will be saved by beauty," Dostoevsky wrote in *The Idiot.*

June 28, 1969, *The Duty of Delight*

We were sitting in the dining room having our morning coffee when Father Roy started to talk to us about the love of God and what it should mean in our lives. He began with the Sermon on the Mount, holding us spellbound, so glowing was his talk, so heartfelt. . . .

Father Roy talked to us of nature and the supernatural, how God became man that man might become God, how we were under the obligation of putting off the old man and putting on Christ, how we had been made the sons of God, by the seed of supernatural life planted in us at our baptism, and of the necessity we were under to see that the seed grew and flourished. We had to aim at perfection; we had to be guided by the folly of the Cross.

He not only pointed out to us the obligation we were under by the vows we had taken at our baptism to put off the world, the flesh, and the devil, but he pointed out the means to do this by what he called acting always for the "supernatural motive"—"*moteef,*" he pronounced it—in this way supernaturalizing all our actions of every day. If we did our works of mercy to be praised by men, or from pride and vanity and sense of power, then we had had our reward. If we did them for the love of God, in whose image man had been made, then God would reward us; then we were doing them for a supernatural motive. There was little freedom in this life, except in the realm of motive or intention. We could do things either because we were compelled to, or because we loved God and wanted to. And never mind, if we did not by our own sacrifice put off the old man and put on the new; God would see to it that we did so in the natural course of events, just as we grew in age, losing little by little our sense of life, our eyesight, our teeth, our hearing. "Oh, yes, we would be stripped," he laughed gaily. "God so loved the world," he cried out with a thrill in his voice. God was that Hound of Heaven who would pursue us, who would not let us go. . . .

As Peter [Maurin] always dealt with the things of this world, so Father Roy always dealt with the things of the next, but the two were interwoven; time and eternity were one. As St. Catherine [of Siena] said, "All the way to heaven is heaven," because He had said, "I am the way." We were like workers for a Utopia already living in their Utopia. We were dying and yet we lived. Were in sorrow yet rejoicing.

The Long Loneliness

One might say that the retreat given at the farm at Easton these last three years, and now is given at Newburgh, New York, is a basic retreat in that it makes man realize and face even with despair the work that is before him, the death to self, the chasm he must bridge, to reach God. We must begin sometime to aim at sanctity. The tragedy, Newman said, is never to begin. Or having put one's hand to the plough, to turn back. To become a tired radical. To settle down to relish comfortably past performances of self-sacrifice and self-denial. It is not enough, St. Ambrose remarks, to leave all our possessions, we must also follow Him, and that means to the Cross, to Gethsemane and Calvary, before one can share in the Resurrection and Ascension.

"I die daily," St. Paul said, and I've often thought it was not the big struggles, the great deaths we have to undergo that are so hard, as the daily torture of denying oneself, mortifying, putting to death the old man in us. Thank God a good part is done *for us*. . . .

Seven years have passed since the beginning of the basic retreat, and we have died many deaths, and many sorrows have entered our lives. Not only the tragedy of a great war, a cataclysm that brought with it the atom bomb and an apocalyptic attitude toward life, but also all the small tragedies which make up our lives. . . .

But the daily tragedies of life, of poverty, and loss of love, and sickness and death, striking in our midst; these are the sorrows and pain incident to dying daily, to putting off the old man and putting on Christ. Dying is not pleasant. Dying is painful. We have to accept the Cross, take up our Cross, and die to rise again. It is growth, normal growth, and if the egg does not proceed in due course to become a chick and put on wings, it becomes a rotten egg.

Youth demands the heroic, Claudel says, and the heroic is the tragic, and the glorious, the laying down one's life for one's brother, the losing it to save it, the following of Christ, not just the giving-up of possessions.

Youth in this era has begun to know about what the heroic is, and has through war and revolution endured sacrifice, poverty, cold and hunger, grim pain and imprisonment, loss of all worldly goods. We cannot deny the heroism of the world, of countless thousands of those who took part in the last gigantic slaughter, of men and women who laid down their lives, "who gave their all." And despite the exalted mouthings of hired writers for the government, we know with that we would be happy if we were as sure of our courage as the unknown and unsung heroes throughout the world that have risen up in this day.

But we know too, that heroism can go much further, that there is a martyrdom of the inner senses, the understanding and the will; that until we see the kenotic aspects of Christ's life, the humiliations of his manhood, the scorn heaped upon him; until we understand how little he thought of *worldly* honor and prudence, we have not yet begun to "put on Christ."

Certainly the Catholic Worker has failed—both in establishing Houses of Hospitality as Peter envisioned them, or Farming Communes. We have succeeded in many small ways, hidden ways, and influenced the lives, we well know, of countless thousands and by the paper and by *all efforts which have failed.* We have sowed in tears, and others will reap in joy. "Have you aimed at failure?" someone asked once. No, we have seen no reason why these ideas expressed by Peter and others in *The Catholic Worker* should not work out to build up a new society within the shell of the old. God did not mean that life should be so difficult. He has provided enough for all, and man in his greed has made a mess of things. I'm firmly convinced that we should keep the vision Peter has held up to us, work towards it, recognizing with humility our mistakes and the gains of others, and appreciating all the means the Church has held out to us.

We have a tremendous work before us—to live and to die in love of Christ. So let us all begin again, our readers, our fellow workers, and pray that God will raise up more apostles for the vineyard who will follow in the footsteps of the "humiliated Christ."

July–August 1947

What was it that we were taken with in the retreat? Of course it was stimulating, glowing alive, challenging. . . .

For too long, too little has been expected of us. When Christ spoke, He spoke from the Mount to the multitudes. He called on all men to take up their cross and follow Him. When we listened to Fr. Lacouture's retreat, we began to understand the distinction between nature and the supernatural . . . and saw for the first time the incomparable heights to which man is called. We saw for the first time man's spiritual capacities, raised as he is to be a child of God. We saw the basis of our dignity.

I could write a great deal about that retreat, and all it brought to us, the new vistas which opened out before us. But I will simply say that it gave us spiritual direction. We were learning how to die to ourselves, to live in Christ, and all the turmoil of the movement, all the pruning of natural love, all the disappointments were explained by the doctrine of the Cross, in the folly of the Cross. The retreat gave us hope and courage. . . . We feel that we have been participants of a great spiritual movement which is still going on, though it is perhaps now in the shadow. The seed has fallen into the ground and died. But we know that it will bear fruit.

December 1951

Rabbi Abraham Heschel said at the Liturgical Conference in Milwaukee that what we needed, what the world needed, was prayer.

And now I pick up Thomas Merton's last book, *Contemplative Prayer,* which I am starting to read, and the foreword by our good Quaker friend Douglas Steere brought back to my memory a strange incident in my life. He quotes William Blake: "We are put on earth for a little space that we may learn to bear the beams of love." And he goes on to say that to escape these beams, to protect ourselves from these beams, even devout men hasten to devise protective clothing. We do not want to be irradiated by love.

Suddenly I remembered coming home from a meeting in Brooklyn many years ago, sitting in an uncomfortable bus seat facing a few poor people. One of them, a downcast, ragged man, suddenly epitomized for me the desolation, the hopelessness of the destitute, and I began to weep. I had been struck by one of those "beams of love," wounded by it in a most particular way. It was my own condition that I was weeping about—my own hardness of heart, my own sinfulness. I recognized this as a moment of truth, an experience of what the *New Catechism* calls our "tremendous, universal, inevitable and yet inexcusable incapacity to love." I had not read that line when I had that experience, but that is what I felt. I think that ever since then I have prayed sincerely those scriptural verses, "Take away my heart of stone and give me a heart of flesh." I had been using this prayer as one of the three acts of faith, hope, and charity: "I believe, help my unbelief." "In Thee have I hoped, let me never be confounded." "Take away my heart of stone and give me a heart of flesh," so that I may learn how to truly love my brother because in him, in his meanest guise, I am encountering Christ.

Perhaps I knew in that moment in the bus in Brooklyn what St. Augustine meant when he cried out, "May I know myself so that I may know Thee." Because I felt so strongly my nothingness, my powerlessness to do anything about this horrifying recognition of my own hardness of heart, it drove me to the recognition that in God alone was my strength. Without Him I could do nothing. Yet I could do all things in Him who strengthened me. So there was happiness there, too. The tears were of joy as well as grief.

"Adventures in Prayer,"
The Third Hour, 1970, *Selected Writings*

3

AT HOME IN THE CHURCH

From the time of her conversion until her death, Dorothy never ceased to express her love for the Church and gratitude for the faith that was given her. She wrote, "Gratitude brought me into the Church and that gratitude grows, and the first word my heart will utter, when I face my God, is 'Thanks.'"

Yet, her love for the Church always left room for a clear-eyed apprehension of its sins and failings. As she wrote in The Long Loneliness, *"I loved the Church for Christ made visible. Not for itself, because it was so often a scandal to me. Romano Guardini said the Church is the Cross on which Christ was crucified; one could not separate Christ from His Cross, and one must live in a state of permanent dissatisfaction with the Church. . . ."*

Dorothy counted the Eucharist among the greatest gifts of the Church. She attended daily Mass, and often wrote that without this and Scripture she would not be able to continue. The presence of Christ in the bread and wine of Communion was connected also to her recognition of the Body of Christ in the poor, and in the experience of community and hospitality. Every day on the soup line she was reminded of the disciples on the road to Emmaus who recognized Christ "in the breaking of bread."

I know now that the Catholic Church is the church of the poor, no matter what you say about the wealth of her priests and bishops. I have mentioned in these pages the few Catholics I met before my conversion, but daily I saw people coming from Mass. Never did I set foot in a Catholic church but that I saw people there at home with Him. First Fridays, novenas, and missions brought the masses thronging in and out of the Catholic churches. They were of all nationalities, of all classes, but most of all they were the poor. The very attacks made against the Church proved her Divinity to me. Nothing but a Divine institution could have survived the betrayal of Judas, the denial of Peter, the sins of many of those who professed her Faith, who were supposed to minister to her poor.

From Union Square to Rome

I am sure that it is because the Church is so alert to Man, as body and soul, because she believes in the resurrection of the body and life everlasting, that I became strongly attracted to her when I began to catch glimpses of her later.

Even the garishness of her beauty appealed to me and still does. Stained-glass windows, statues, flowers, and pure beeswax candles, incense, the organ and the choir when they have them, all these appeals to the senses contribute to devotion and the sense of mystery and awe. I enjoy even the feel of a rosary between my fingers, whether it is a wooden Indian one, an amber Moslem one, or a Russian woolen one, or our own Roman Catholic variety. To finger it, to let all my distractions turn to prayers for the people I am thinking of, even these distractions come from repeating the mystery to be meditated on.

October 1970

I would like to impress upon you how I feel about the Church. Of course conscience comes first, but just the same, nothing would ever drive me from the Church. No pronouncement from the Pope or the Bishops, no matter how wrong I thought them, would cause me to leave the Church. I would rather stop the work, keep silent and wait. The spiritual weapons of prayer and sufferings would do more to further any cause than protest and defiance. God writes straight with crooked lines, and arrogance and pride would do more to wreck a cause than any pronouncement from the hierarchy.

> To Ammon Hennacy, September 1950,
> *All the Way to Heaven*

When Pope John was journeying in North Africa before he was made a Cardinal, he wrote that his trip brought home to him vividly "the problem of the conversion of the people without the faith. The whole life and purpose of the Church, of the priesthood, of true and good diplomacy is there: Give me souls: take all the rest."

And I thought to myself, "We are the Church too, we the laity," and this is our problem also. This is why we are opposing war, and right now the war in Vietnam. Souls are being lost. War is a sin against Love, against life. God is Love, and he wills that all men be saved. The whole purpose of our life is Love. Why did God create us? Because He loved us. Why do we love him? Because He first loved us. And God so loved the world that He gave his only begotten Son to us, to show us our salvation, knowing that in the exercise of our freedom we were going to continue to crucify Him to the end of the world. We are doing it now in Vietnam, in the death of every man, woman, and child. "Inasmuch as ye have done it unto the least of these my brethren ye have done it unto me."

September 1965

THE BREAD OF LIFE

Thank God for the sacraments, the food of life which we can receive to strengthen us. Thank God for the Word made flesh and for the Word in the Scriptures. Thank God for the Gospel which St. Thérèse pinned close to her heart, and which the murderer Raskolnikov [in *Crime and Punishment*] listened to from the lips of a prostitute and took with him into the Siberian prison. The Word is our light and our understanding, and it is also our food.

Ave Maria, December 3, 1966,
Selected Writings

We are not, most of us, capable of exalted emotion, save rarely. We are not capable always of feelings of love, awe, gratitude, and repentance. So Christ has taken the form of bread that we may more readily approach Him, and feeding daily, assimilating Christ so that it is not we but Christ working in us, we may be made more capable of understanding and realizing and loving Him.

Yes, in bread Christ has become so simple—has condescended so far that a child can eat the Sacred Food with love and gratitude. . . .

There is the question, why did Christ institute this Sacrament of His Body and Blood? And the answer is very simple. It was because He loved us and wished to be with us. "My delights are to be with the children of men." He made us and He loves us. His presence in the Blessed Sacrament is the great proof of that love. . . .

It took me a long time as a convert to realize the presence of Christ as Man in the Sacrament. He is the same Jesus Who walked on earth, Who slept in the boat as the tempest arose, Who hungered in the desert, Who prayed in the garden, Who conversed with the woman by the well, Who rested at the house of Martha and Mary, Who wandered through the cornfields, picking the ears of corn to eat.

Jesus is there as Man. He is there, Flesh and Blood, Soul and Divinity. He is our leader Who is always with us. Do you wonder that Catholics are exultant in this knowledge, that their Leader is with them? "I am with you all days, even to the consummation of the world."

Christ is bread on our altars because bread is the staple of the world, the simplest thing in the world, something of which we eat and never get tired. We will always have bread whether it is corn, wheat, or rye, or whatever it is made from. We will always find wherever we go some staple which is called bread.

We eat to sustain life. It is the most elemental thing we do. For the life of the body we need food. For the life of the soul we need food. So the simplest, most loving, most thorough thing Christ could do before He died, was to institute the Blessed Sacrament. He did this by taking a piece of bread which He blessed and broke and gave to his disciples saying, "Take ye and eat. This is My Body." And taking the chalice He gave thanks, and gave to them saying: "Drink ye all of this for This is My Blood." And He told them to do this in commemoration of Him.

If you sat and thought forever and ever, you could not think of any way for Christ to remain with us which would bring us closer to Him. I could keep on writing and writing and never come to the end of this, but I won't. I only hope that in your sincerity, which acknowledges my sincerity, you will read me through. You know how much emphasis Christ put on the "little ones" who are the majority. Not only the children, but the poor and helpless. Those without learning, when it comes to reading books about the Blessed Sacrament or dialectical materialism, are another instance of what I mean.

With all my writing to you the products of my thought on this subject, I can only end with the words of Jesus, "I thank Thee, O Father, Lord of heaven and earth, that thou hast hid these things from the wise and prudent, and hast revealed them unto babes: Even so, Father. For so it seemed good in thy sight."

For so it seemed good in His sight!

From Union Square to Rome

The Second Vatican Council and the Mass

We laymen have said little so far about the coming Council and Christian renewal. Partly it is because as lay people expressing ourselves at all times about such important issues as man's work, his present unemployment, the situation of the family, materialistic education in Catholic school as well as public school, man and the state, war and peace—it is endless, the issues we have covered, the articles we have written over almost thirty years. One might say we were preparing the ground, pointing up the issues.

This is probably my last chance, this issue of the *Catholic Worker*, for me personally to write about some things that are in my heart about the Mass, for instance, that holy sacrifice, which is the heart of our life, bringing us into the closest of all contacts with our Lord Jesus Christ, enabling us literally to "put on Christ," as St. Paul said, and to begin to say with him, "Now, not I live, but Jesus Christ in me." With a strong consciousness of this, we remember too those lines, "Without Me, ye can do nothing," and "with Me you can do all things." . . . How inadequate words are to say these things, to write them. . . .

But the Mass begins our day, it is our food and drink, our delight, our refreshment, our courage, our light. And it is our Mass, not just the priest's Mass. . . .

And now we come to our real criticism, the point of all this that I am trying to write. Most priests rush through the Mass as though they were going to forget the words unless they say them as fast as possible. Not only the Latin which is garbled so that it sounds like magic, but also the vernacular, the prayers at the foot of the altar. In those prayers we do have the vernacular and all the priests who are crying aloud for the vernacular do not seem to realize that those prayers they are saying are important too, and the intention with which those prayers are said. . . .

With this recognition of the importance of the Word made flesh and dwelling among us, still with us in the bread and wine of the altar, how can any priest tear through the Mass as though it were a repetitious duty? This is the impression they give people when they do this, like the children at Fatima who used to say only Hail Mary, or Our Father, and think they had said their prayers, and perhaps they had if they realized the holiness of these words. The priest often says the first words and slides through the rest in meaningless mutter. And some of the best priests I have met do this, abusing the prayers of the Mass in this way.

I am begging them not to. I am begging them to speak as though the words were holy and inspired and with power in themselves to produce in us the understanding—the participation that should change our lives.

"You cannot fail to see the power of mere words," Joseph Conrad wrote in his preface to *A Personal Record*. "Such words as Glory, for instance, or Pity. Shouted with perseverance, with ardor, with conviction, these two by their sound alone, have set whole nations in motion and upheaved the dry hard ground on which rests our whole social fabric."

So I am praying that at the Council, at all the Masses and at the Council, the word made flesh will be among them. Forsake them not O Lord, Our God.

September 1962

They Knew Him in the Breaking of Bread

In this article Dorothy described an incident that has become steeped in legend. She writes with disapproval of a priest who said Mass at the Catholic Worker using a coffee cup in place of a chalice. According to pious accounts of this story, Dorothy supposedly insisted that the cup be buried in the soil behind St. Joseph House. In fact, as she recounts in her article, "I was not there when this happened," but only heard about it later. And while she was saddened by anything that seemed lacking in proper reverence for Christ's Body and Blood, her reflection prompted a surprising second thought: "And yet—and yet—perhaps it happened to remind us that the power of God did not rest on all these appurtenances with which we surround it."

A ragged old man with a sandwich in his pocket came in and sat in the back of the church this morning. One of the parishioners who had just been to communion started shooing him out. "He is smoking!" she said, shaking her head. "Don't you smoke in here," and she was like a little mother hen driving him before her.

It was raining outside and there was no park bench on which to rest. He was either sleeping in some vacant house or at the Municipal lodging house on Third Street half a dozen blocks away and was put out early in the morning with his sandwich. Perhaps he did not know he was in church. Peter Maurin in his last five years lost his mind and got lost himself in city and country, and even in the house of hospitality itself. Sometimes he did not even know where he was supposed to sleep. He was truly poor.

I was writing in church myself when this little incident occurred and perhaps to the purist I too should have been put out. But I was trying to put down my problems of this immediate present, hoping that it would help me solve them or make a beginning. Often I have done this, only to find six months later that the problems had somehow disappeared.

But to try to face up to some of my problems: The incident of the man smoking in church leads me to one of the problems but perhaps a most basic one: the lack of the reverence and respect that we should have for holy things, and for all men as creatures of God. God, the Father, created us and all the universe, so all things are holy. One may laugh for joy, but not in derision. . . .

I suppose I am rambling because I hate to get to the point, and that point is that I am afraid I am a traditionalist, in that I do not like to see Mass offered with a large coffee cup as a chalice. I suppose I am romantic too, since I loved the Arthur legend as a child and reverenced the Holy Grail and the search for it. I feel with Newman that my faith is founded on a creed, as Rev. Louis Bouyer wrote of Newman in that magnificent biography of his.

"I believe in God, Father Almighty, Creator of heaven and earth. And of all things visible and invisible, and in His Only Son Jesus Christ, our Lord."

I believe too that when the priest offers Mass at the altar, and says the solemn words, "This is my body, this is my blood," that the bread and the wine truly become the body and blood of Christ, Son of God, one of the Three Divine persons. I believe in a personal God. I believe in Jesus Christ, true God and true man. And intimate, oh how most closely intimate we may desire to be, I believe we must render most reverent homage to Him who created us and stilled the sea and told the winds to be calm, and multiplied the loaves and fishes. He is transcendent and He is immanent. He is closer than the air we breathe and just as vital to us. I speak impetuously, from my heart, and if I err theologically in my expression, I beg forgiveness. . . .

To me the Mass, high or low, is glorious and I feel that though we know we are but dust, at the same time we know too, and most surely through the Mass that we are little less than the angels, that indeed it is now not I but Christ in me worshiping, and in Him I can do all things, though without Him I am nothing. I would not dare write or speak or try to follow the vocation God has given me to work for the poor and for peace, if I did not have this constant reassurance of the Mass, the confidence the Mass gives. (The very word confidence means "with faith.")

It is one thing for a Father Ciszek to offer Mass, to conse-crate the wine in a coffee cup in the prison camps of Siberia. It is quite another thing to have this happen in New York. And yet—and yet—perhaps it happened to remind us that the power of God did not rest on all these appurtenances with which we surround it. That all over the world, in the jungles of South America and Vietnam and Africa—all the troubled, indeed anguished spots of the world—there Christ is with the poor, the suffering, even in the cup we share together, in the bread we eat. "They knew Him in the breaking of bread."

March 1966

Bread for the Hungry

In 1976 Dorothy was honored to speak at the Eucharistic Congress in Philadelphia. The date was August 6, the Feast of the Trans-figuration, but also the anniversary of the dropping of the atomic bomb on Hiroshima. She was disturbed to learn that the bishops had scheduled for this day a Mass for the Armed Forces. Members of the Catholic Worker and other pacifists planned to pass out leaflets as a reminder. Though Dorothy rarely wrote out a speech, on this occasion she did and it was published in the paper. The strain of her divided feelings may have contributed to a subsequent heart attack. It would be her last public speech.

My conversion began many years ago, at a time when the material world around me began to speak in my heart of the love of God. There is a beautiful passage in St. Augustine, whose *Confessions* I read at this time. "What is it I love when I love Thee," it begins, and goes on to list all the material beauty and enjoyment to be found in the life of the senses. The sea, which surrounded us, rather, it was a bay leading out to sea, provided food, fish, and shellfish in abundance, even the seaweeds, which a Japanese friend told me were part of the food of her people. Our garden grew vegetables; the fields berries, the trees fruits. Everything spoke to me of a Creator who satisfied all our hungers.

It was also the physical aspect of the Church which attracted me. Bread and wine, water (all water is made holy since Christ was baptized in the Jordan), incense, the sound of waves and wind, all nature cried out to me.

My love and gratitude to the Church have grown through the years. She was my mother and nourished me, and taught me.

She taught me the crowning love of the life of the Spirit. But she also taught me that "before we bring our gifts of service, of gratitude, to the altar—if our brother have anything against us, we must hesitate to approach the altar to receive the Eucharist."

"Unless you do penance, you shall all perish." Penance comes before the Eucharist. Otherwise we partake of the Sacrament unworthily.

And here we are on August 6th, the day the first atomic bomb was dropped, which ended the Second World War. There had been holocausts before—massacres, after the First World War, of the Armenians, all but forgotten now, and the holocaust of the Jews, God's chosen people. When He came to earth as Man, He chose them. And He told us, "All men are brothers," and that it was His will that all men be saved. Japanese, Jew, Armenian.

It is a fearful thought, that unless we do penance, we will perish.

Our Creator gave us life, and the Eucharist to sustain our life.

But we have given the world instruments of *death* of inconceivable magnitude.

Today, we are celebrating—how strange to use such a word—a Mass for the military, the "armed forces." No-one in charge of the Eucharistic Congress had remembered what *August 6th* means in the minds of all who are dedicated to the work of peace.

Why not a Mass for the military on some other day? Antoine St. Exupéry, a flyer in World War II and the author of *Wind, Sand and Stars*, tells of the feeling men at war have for each other—the sense of being united in a common cause, "a readiness to give all, *to lay down one's life*." Such expressions are used in all sincerity.

And who does not love bands, and the discipline of marching men, and the banners!

I, myself, had grandparents who fought in the Civil War—on opposite sides, however, and animosities remained between families in my childhood. My two brothers were in the First World War and one in World War II, and my grandson was in our most recent war, when he was in the jungles in Vietnam, in the small bands who went out "to search and destroy." Women, who were born to nourish, to bring forth life, not to destroy it, must do more than thank God we survived it.

I plead, in this short paper, that we will regard that military Mass, and all our Masses today, as an act of penance, begging God to forgive us. I am gratified for the opportunity given me at this Congress to express myself in this way. I thank God for the freedom of Holy Mother Church.

I must not forget Ammon Hennacy, who died in 1970, one of the old editors of *The Catholic Worker*, who, since Hiroshima and Nagasaki, fasted from all food, solid or liquid, allowing himself only water, giving a day of this penance for every year since the bombs were dropped.

If he were with us today, he would be fasting over thirty days. The last years of his life he fasted, carrying a picket sign all day in the hot sun, in front of some Federal building, in whatever city he happened to be living. He died in Salt Lake City after a heart attack, which occurred during another picketing, protesting the execution of two young men in Utah. Ammon reverenced life.

Today, some of the young pacifists giving out leaflets here are fasting, as a personal act of penance for the sin of our country, which we love.

September 1976

THE CROSS ON WHICH CHRIST WAS CRUCIFIED

Obedience

On the one hand there is the question of obedience. On the other hand there is neglect of the poor, a lack of understanding concerning the needy and the poor. Which sin is the greater? Practically everyone would say the second, because everybody gives lip service to the poor when they don't give hand or foot service. But the question of obedience goes back still further, "to man's first disobedience," and to that great obedience, the folly of the cross, "He was obedient unto death." And on just such obedience, such a folly of love, stands the very life of the Church, and the Church is the Body of Christ, which we love. Though the members rend each other in wars and dissensions, still there is no separation of the head from the members, and to love the one is to love the other.

Americans hate the word obedience, and the only way to look at it is from the supernatural point of view, not from the natural, because it is often folly. This is not to deny that conscience comes first: one must obey the voice of conscience, one must obey God rather than men, as St. Peter himself was the first to say.

And here is one of those delicate problems that drive the rest of the world crazy when they observe the Catholic in his relations to Holy Mother the Church. They point out the scandals in the Church, the mistakes in history, the bad Popes, the Inquisition, the lining up of the Church with temporal power, the concordats, the expediency, the diplomacy, and so on and so on.

Right under one's nose there is always plenty to complain of. Churches, schools, monasteries being built while the municipal lodging house is packed with mothers and children separated from husbands and fathers because of lack of housing; a spreading unemployment; race prejudice amongst Catholics, and priests and sisters, too; anti-Semitism—oh, yes, there is plenty of scandal.

"The just will be judged first," and the "just" is made up of the lame, the halt and the blind because Christ came to call sinners, and the Church is full of them, in high and low places.

Guardini said that the Church was the Cross and one could not separate Christ from his Cross. He said, too, that we must learn to live in a state of permanent dissatisfaction and impatience with the Church. We have to suffer and hang our heads at all the accusations made against us. We are all guilty, we all make up the Body of Christ. And we must suffer with bitterness, the Little Flower said, if need be, and without courage, and that is what makes the suffering especially keen.

E. I. Watkin's essay on clerical materialism in *The Catholic Center* is a good illustration of the trouble of the day. And it is a trouble indeed. Believing as we do in the Mystical Body of Christ, for every expensive convent and monastery and school and rectory being built in this country, for every luxury which has come to be considered a necessity by our people in America, we may hold ourselves responsible for the persecution of priests and nuns in other parts of the world. And I do know that the great mass of priests and seminarians and nuns look upon them as the lucky ones who are counted worthy to shed their blood for Christ.

Persecution is deserved and undeserved. "And it must needs be that scandals come but woe to those by whom they come." "Woe to the shepherds that feed themselves and not their sheep."

. . . We recognize and accept the authority of the Church as we do that of Christ himself. Our Holy Father the Pope is our dear sweet Christ on earth, as St. Catherine called him, even when she was pointing out with the liberty of a saint, how wrong he was at the time, in his conduct of temporal affairs.

We accept the authority of the Church but we wonder why it shows itself in such strange ways. . . .

We are obliged to conform to Christ even in Christ's folly. He submitted to the injustices, the mistakes, the crimes committed against Him, and against St. John the Baptist. He submitted even to be termed a lamb led to the slaughter, and He was King of the whole world.

December 1949

The Meaning of Poverty

I am thinking of how many leave the Church because of the scandal of the wealth of the Church, the luxury of the Church which began in the very earliest day, even perhaps when the Apostles debated on which should be highest in the kingdom and when the poor began quarreling as to who were receiving the most from the common table, the Greek Jews or the Jerusalem Jews. St. Paul commented on the lack of esteem for the poor, and the kowtowing to the rich, and St. John in the Apocalypse spoke of the scandal of the churches "where charity had grown cold."

It has always been this way in the Church. On the one hand the struggle for detachment, to grow in the supernatural life which seems so unnatural at times, when the vision is dim.

Thank God for the sacraments, the food of life which we can receive to strengthen us. Thank God for the Word made flesh and for the Word in the Scriptures. Thank God for the Gospel which St. Thérèse pinned close to her heart, and which the murderer Raskolnikov listened to from the lips of a prostitute and took with him into the Siberian prison. The Word is our light and our understanding, and it is also our food.

Ave Maria, December 3, 1966, *Selected Writings*

In Peace Is My Bitterness Most Bitter

This reflection was prompted by the outspoken support of many bishops, including Dorothy's own archbishop, Cardinal Spellman, for the war in Vietnam. She reflected on the fact that "Our worst enemies are those of our own household."

It is not just Vietnam, it is South Africa, it is Nigeria, the Congo, Indonesia, all of Latin America. It is not just the pictures of all the women and children who have been burnt alive in Vietnam, or the men who have been tortured, and died. It is not just the headless victims of the war in Colombia. It is not just the words of Cardinal Spellman and Archbishop Hannan. It is the fact that whether we like it or not, we are Americans. It is indeed our country, right or wrong, as the Cardinal said in another context. We are warm and fed and secure (aside from occasional muggings and murders amongst us). We are the nation the most powerful, the most armed and we are supplying arms and money to the rest of the world where we are not ourselves fighting. We are eating while there is famine in the world.

Scripture tells us that the picture of judgment presented to us by Jesus is of Dives sitting and feasting with his friends while Lazarus sat hungry at the gate, the dogs, the scavengers of the East, licking his sores. We are Dives. Woe to the rich! *We* are the rich. The works of mercy are the opposite of the works of war, feeding the hungry, sheltering the homeless, nursing the sick, visiting the prisoner. But we are destroying crops, setting fire to entire villages and to the people in them. We are not performing the works of mercy but the works of war. We cannot repeat this enough.

When the apostles wanted to call down fire from heaven on the inhospitable Samaritans, the "enemies" of the Jews, Jesus said to them, "You know not of what Spirit you are." When Peter told our Lord not to accept the way of the Cross and His own death, He said, "Get behind me, Satan. For you are not on the side of God but of men." But He also had said, "Thou are Peter and upon this rock I will build my church." Peter denied Jesus three times at that time in history, but after the death on the cross, and the Resurrection and the Descent of the Holy Spirit, Peter faced up to Church and

State alike and said, "We must obey God rather than men." Deliver us, O Lord, from the fear of our enemies, which makes cowards of us all.

I can sit in the presence of the Blessed Sacrament and wrestle for that peace in the bitterness of my soul, a bitterness which many Catholics throughout the world feel, and I can find many things in Scripture to console me, to change my heart from hatred to love of enemy. "Our worst enemies are those of our own household," Jesus said. Picking up the Scriptures at random (as St. Francis used to do), I read about Peter, James, and John who went up on the Mount of Transfiguration and saw Jesus talking with Moses and Elias, transfigured before their eyes. (A hint of the life to come, Maritain said.) Jesus transfigured! He who was the despised of men, no beauty in him, spat upon, beaten, dragged to his cruel death on the way to the cross! A man so much like other men that it took the kiss of a Judas to single him out from the others when the soldiers, so closely allied to the priests, came to take him. Reading this story of the Transfiguration, the words stood out, words foolishly babbled, about the first building project of the Church, proposed by Peter. "Lord shall we make here three shelters, one for you, one for Moses and one for Elias?" And the account continues, "For he did not know what to say, he was so terrified."

Maybe they are terrified, these princes of the church, as we are often terrified at the sight of violence, which is present every now and then in our houses of hospitality, and which is always a threat in the streets of the slums. I have often thought it is a brave thing to do, these Christmas visits of Cardinal Spellman to the American troops all over the world, Europe, Korea, Vietnam. But oh, God what are all these Americans, so-called Christians doing all over the world so far from our own shores?

But what words are those he spoke—going against even the Pope, calling for victory, total victory? Words are as strong and powerful as bombs, as napalm. How much the government counts on those words, pays for those words to exalt our own way of life, to build up fear of the enemy. Deliver us, Lord, from the *fear* of the enemy. That is one of the lines in the psalms, and we are not asking God to deliver us from enemies but from the fear of them. Love casts out fear, but we have to get over the fear in order to get close enough to love them.

There is plenty to do, for each one of us, working on our own hearts, changing our own attitudes, in our own neighborhoods. If the just man falls seven times daily, we each one of us fall more than that in thought, word, and deed. Prayer and fasting, taking up our own cross daily and following Him, doing penance, these are the hard words of the Gospel.

As to the Church, where else shall we go, except to the Bride of Christ, one flesh with Christ? Though she is a harlot at times, she is our Mother. We should read the Book of Hosea, which is a picture of God's steadfast love not only for the Jews, His chosen people, but for His Church, of which we are every one of us members or potential members. Since there is no time with God, we are all one, all one body, Chinese, Russians, Vietnamese, and He has *commanded us to love one another.*

"A new commandment I give, that you love others as I have loved you," not to the defending of your life, but to the laying down of your life.

A hard saying.

Love is indeed a "harsh and dreadful thing" to ask of us, of each one of us, but it is the only answer.

January 1967

4

CALLED TO BE SAINTS

It would be hard to exaggerate the role that saints played in the life of Dorothy Day and the origins of the Catholic Worker. Peter Maurin told her that the best way to study Catholic history was through the saints—those who most faithfully embodied the spirit of Christ. Constantly she invoked the saints as patrons and intercessors, "picketing" before St. Joseph when funds ran dry, calling on the assistance of the Blessed Mother in coping with the problems in her Catholic Worker family, remembering the "perfect joy" of St. Francis whenever there was an occasion to share some portion of unmerited suffering.

In its early years The Catholic Worker *was largely illustrated with Ade Bethune's images of the saints. Depicted in modern dress, engaged in the works of mercy or ordinary work, these figures literally illustrated what the editors were trying to communicate through words and actions. The saints were our friends and companions, examples of the gospel in action.*

While discussing the saints, Dorothy always acknowledged their humanity, their capacity for discouragement and sorrow, their mistakes and failures, along with their courage and faithfulness. There is no doubt she wished to take them off their pedestals, to show them as real human beings who nevertheless represented in their time the ideals and spirit of the gospel. She felt it was important that we tell the stories of "saints as they really were, as they affected the lives of their times." But it was also important to underscore their radical challenge: how St. Catherine of Siena confronted the pope; how St. Benedict promoted the spirit of peace; how St. Francis met with the sultan in a mission of reconciliation. Whenever she felt discouragement about Church leaders, she remembered: "In all history popes and bishops and father abbots seem to have been blind and power loving and greedy. I never expected leadership from them. It is the saints that keep appearing all through history who keep things going."

But above all, Dorothy believed that the canonized saints were those who reminded us of our true vocation. "We are all called to be saints," she wrote, "and we might as well get over our bourgeois fear of the name." To be a saint was to answer our original calling, to put off the old person and put on Christ. And yet she also acknowledged the need for a wider understanding of saints and holiness. Even in her youth she had asked herself the question, "Where were the saints to change the social order? Not just to minister to the slaves but to do away with slavery?"

Dorothy's own list of faithful witnesses extended beyond the officially canonized saints of the Church. They included writers, artists, peacemakers, fictional characters from novels by Ignazio Silone and Dostoevsky, and what she called "saint-revolutionists"—those, including "nonbelievers," who laid down their lives in the spirit of solidarity, or in the cause of peace and justice. She did not hesitate to name the Hindu Mahatma Gandhi, the "Great Soul" of India, as one of the most important saints of our time.

Her constant prayer was for more saints—"big saints and little saints"—and to be attentive to the holiness of those in our midst. "Sometimes we don't see them around us, sometimes their sanctity is obscured by the human, but they are there nonetheless."

EARLY ENCOUNTERS

Childhood Memories

The Harrington family also lived in that block of tenements, and there were nine children, the eldest a little girl of twelve. She was a hard-working little girl, and naturally I had the greatest admiration for her on account of the rigorous life she lived. I had a longing then, I remember, for the rigorous life. I was eight, and I had begun to help my mother for the first time. . . .

But I had a tremendous amount of liberty compared to little Mary Harrington, my senior. It was not until after the dishes were done that she could come out to play in the evening. Often she was so tired that we just stretched out on the long back porch, open to the sky. We lay there gazing up at the only beauty that the city had to offer us, and we talked and dreamed.

I don't remember what we talked about, but I do remember one occasion when she told me of the life of some saint. I don't remember which one, nor can I remember any of the incidents of it. I can only remember the feeling of lofty enthusiasm I had, how my heart seemed almost bursting with desire to take part in such high endeavor. One verse of the Psalms often comes to my mind: "Enlarge thou my heart, O Lord, that Thou mayest enter in." This was one of those occasions when my small heart was enlarged. I could feel it swelling with love and gratitude to such a good God for such a friendship as Mary's, for conversations such as hers, and I was filled with lofty ambitions to be a saint, a natural striving, a thrilling recognition of the possibilities of spiritual adventure.

I, too, wanted to do penance for my own sins and for the sins of the whole world, for I had a keen sense of sin, of natural imperfection and earthliness. I often felt clearly that

I was being deliberately evil in my attitudes, just as I clearly recognized truth when I came across it. And the thrill of joy that again and again stirred my heart when I came across spiritual truth and beauty never abated, never left me as I grew older.

The sad thing is that one comes across it so seldom. Natural goodness, natural beauty, brings joy and a lifting of the spirit, but it is not enough, it is not the same. The special emotions I am speaking of came only at hearing the word of God. It was as though each time I heard Our Lord spoken of, a warm feeling of joy filled me. It was hearing of someone you love and who loves you.

From Union Square to Rome

Rayna Prohme

In later writing about saints Dorothy bemoaned the tendency to see saints as perfect people, or world-disdaining ascetics, close to God but not entirely human. "No wonder no one wants to be a saint," she wrote. And yet, as she had written in her book about St. Thérèse, "the saint is the holy man, the 'whole man,' the integrated man. We all wish to be that." In her memoir From Union Square to Rome, *she devoted an entire chapter to Rayna Prohme, a nonbeliever born to a Jewish family, who yet exhibited such an example of aliveness, purity, and "spiritual energy" that Dorothy felt ennobled by their friendship. Ultimately, they pursued very different paths. While Dorothy was becoming a Catholic, Rayna, by then a dedicated Communist, was dying of typhoid in Russia. She never ceased to remember and pray for her friend.*

Rayna's joyousness came because she saw always what was noble and beautiful in life and she was happy in it. And I can see now, how being a Communist brought out this spirit in her even more.

Her other trait that [Vincent] Sheean emphasized was her love of truth and I am sure that it was that love which, if she had lived, would have forced her to give up the Communist Party. He told that when he was interviewing her she expressed her great distaste for the "lying" that Communist propaganda makes necessary. She told him that when she could not tell the truth, she preferred to remain silent. I do not think she would have made a very good propagandist, no matter how many years she spent in the Lenin Institute. What I wish to bring out is the positiveness of these virtues, these natural virtues.

Most young people think of virtue as something negative. They think that by avoiding sin they are being good. They think of purity as an absence of impurity. They have not committed those sins which they might have committed. Yet we should think certainly of purity as a shining positive virtue, rather than as a negative one—one that makes itself felt, that stands out glowingly. It is the Old Testament that emphasizes the "Thou shalt nots." The New Testament emphasizes the positive virtue of love which comprises all the rest.

Have you not met in your life people who stood out because some virtue shone in them, was predominant? I can remember people whose goodness shone as a positive adornment, which attracted others and filled them with longing. It would be so easy for us if there were more to inspire us as they do.

Rayna's truth stood out as a positive virtue. She was honest, pure, and loving, but above all shone her joyousness and her truth.

Catholics who read this may be surprised at this glowing appraisal of one who did not believe in Christ. I must remind them that in spite of living in the United States, in a so-called Christian nation, there were no Christians whom

Rayna met who could induce her, either by their actions or their words, to believe in the way of the Cross, in the glorified Christ.

Nothing in her reading that was abstruse and philosophical in school brought her the truth. She was hungering for it, she loved it, she searched for it in years of study at the University of Illinois, but she never found it. She thought she had found it in Communism, then she died. And who knows but that just at death she did find it? We cannot tell. She was searching for it. . . .

I always felt that Rayna had those reserves of "spiritual energy" which [Jacques] Maritain speaks of. "It is to be noted," he writes, "that the reserves of spiritual energy that are to be found in human nature may be liberated by preaching and example and set in operation in the hearts of many without any sense of spiritual things other than that which they may find in the concrete experience of the fight for justice here below. . . . It follows from the idea of Catholicity that every just man of non-Christian denomination belongs to the invisible unity of the Church and on this ground only has a title to salvation. . . ."

So reading, my heart is comforted about Rayna, for most assuredly she loved truth and justice.

From Union Square to Rome

A New Kind of Saint

Even as Dorothy was being drawn to the Catholic Church and the example of the saints, she sensed the need for a different type of saint: "not just to minister to the slaves but to do away with slavery."

Whatever I had read as a child about the saints had thrilled me. I could see the nobility of giving one's life for the sick, the maimed, the leper. Priests and Sisters the world over could be working for the little ones of Christ, and my heart stirred at their work. Who could hear of Damien [of Molokai]—and Stevenson made the whole world hear of him—without feeling impelled to thank God that he had made man so noble?

But there was another question in my mind. Why was so much done in remedying the evil instead of avoiding it in the first place? . . . Where were the saints to try to change the social order, not just to minister to the slaves but to do away with slavery?

From Union Square to Rome

FRIENDS AND PATRONS

In providing Dorothy with a "Catholic view of history," Peter Maurin urged her constantly to read the lives of the saints. Not only were they the best representatives of Christianity, but they offered practical wisdom on trusting in God and overcoming discouragement. This extended to the question of how to start a newspaper without any money.

But how were we going to start it?

Peter did not pretend to be practical along these lines. "I enunciate the principles," he declared grandly.

"But where do we get the money?" I asked him, clinging to the "we," though he was making clear his role as theorist.

"In the history of the saints, capital was raised by prayer. God sends you what you need when you need it. You will be able to pay the printer. Just read the lives of the saints."

St. Francis de Sales scattered leaflets like any radical. St. John of God sold newspapers on the streets. We didn't have to do things on a big scale, Peter made it clear.

I had been reading the life of Rose Hawthorne not long

before, how she started what has since become a chain of cancer hospitals in a four-room tenement apartment such as the one I was living in. Why not start a newspaper in the same way? I began to look on our kitchen as an editorial office, my brother as an assistant to write heads and to help with mechanical make-up. Tamar and I could go out to sell papers on the streets.

The Long Loneliness

St. Teresa of Avila

Reading William James's *Varieties of Religious Experience* had acquainted me with the saints, and I had read the life of St. Teresa of Avila and fallen in love with her. She was a mystic and a practical woman, a recluse and a traveler, a cloistered nun and yet most ACTIVE. She liked to read novels when she was a young girl, and she wore a bright red dress when she entered the convent. Once when she was traveling from one part of Spain to another with some other nuns and a priest to start a convent, and their way took them over a stream, she was thrown from her donkey. The story goes that our Lord said to her, "That is how I treat my friends." And she replied, "And that is why You have so few of them." She called life "a night spent at an uncomfortable inn." Once when she was trying to avoid that recreation hour which is set aside in convents for nuns to be together, the others insisted on her joining them, and she took castanets and danced. When older nuns professed themselves shocked, she returned, "One must do things sometimes to make life more bearable." After she was superior she gave directions when the nuns became melancholy, "to feed them steak," and there were other delightful little touches to the story of her life which made me love her and feel close to her. I have since heard a priest friend of ours remark gloomily that one could go to hell imitating the imperfections of the saints, but these little incidents brought out in her biography made her delightfully near to me. So I decided to name my daughter after her.

The Long Loneliness

St. Joseph

Today as I write it is the feast of St. Joseph, our particular patron, since we too have been so hard put to find shelter not only in New York but in other cities where we have houses of hospitality. We have always looked to him as to one who found a home, poor as it was, for Mary and the holy Child. He is a model for the worker, for the craftsman, for the husband and father, and we beg him most especially to guard our newly acquired house on East First Street, named for him. Hideous violence broke out only a few doors away from us this last week between two motorcycle gangs and resulted in the death of one unidentified youth who was found bound and burned to death in a tenement apartment.

St. Joseph, pray for us all. And pray that the spirit of penance will strengthen us to overcome hatred with love. Drug addiction results in such tragedies, and with many alcohol itself is an addiction. To help our brothers let us do without what maddens the heart of man only too often. Drugs are a good to alleviate pain, and on festivals wine gladdens the heart of men. But we see too much of tragedy. Have pity, have pity on the poor around us, and fast from the unnecessary that the destitute may have more.

March 1969

St. Francis

St. Francis was "the little poor man," and none was more joyful than he; yet he began with tears, with fear and trembling, hiding in a cave from his irate father. He had expropriated some of his father's goods (which he considered his rightful inheritance) in order to repair a church and rectory where he meant to live. It was only later that he came to love Lady Poverty. He took it little by little; it seemed to grow on him. Perhaps kissing the leper was the great step that freed him not only from fastidiousness and fear of disease, but from his attachment to worldly goods as well.

Sometimes it takes but one step. We would like to think so. And yet the older I get the more I see that life is made up of many steps, and they are very small affairs, not giant strides. I have "kissed a leper," not once but twice—consciously—and I cannot say I am much the better for it.

The first time was early one morning on the steps of Precious Blood Church. A woman with cancer of the face was begging (beggars are allowed only in the slums), and when I gave her money (no sacrifice on my part but merely passing on alms which someone had given me) she tried to kiss my hand. The only thing I could do was kiss her dirty old face with the gaping hole in it where an eye and a nose had been. It sounds like a heroic deed, but it was not. One gets used to ugliness so quickly. What one averts one's eyes from one day can easily be borne the next when we have learned a little more about love. Nurses know this, and so do mothers.

Another time I was refusing a bed to a drunken prostitute with a huge, toothless, rouged mouth, a nightmare of a mouth. She had been raising a disturbance in the house. I had been remembering how St. Thérèse said that when you had to say no, when you had to refuse anyone anything, you could at least do it so that they went away a bit happier. I had to deny her a bed, but when that woman asked me to kiss her, I did, and it was a loathsome thing, the way she did it. It was scarcely a mark of normal, human affection.

We suffer these things and they fade from memory. But daily, hourly, to give up our own will and possessions, and especially to subordinate our own impulses and wishes to others—these are hard, hard things; and I don't think they ever get any easier. . . .

April 1953

Mohandas Gandhi

Catholics, as a rule, were not encouraged to speak of non-Christians as models of sanctity. Yet Dorothy did not hesitate to speak of the Hindu Mohandas Gandhi, assassinated in 1948, as one who conformed his life to the example of Christ and carried about him "the aura of divinized humanity."

"Greater love than this no man hath—that a man lay down his life for his friends." There is no public figure who has more conformed his life to the life of Jesus Christ than Gandhi; there is no man who has carried about him more consistently the aura of divinized humanity, who has added his sacrifice to the sacrifice of Christ, whose life has had a more fitting end than that of Gandhi. "A prophet is not without honor save in his own country . . . he came into his own and his own did not receive him." The folly of Gandhi's life, the failure of Gandhi's life—it is the folly and failure of the Cross. The failure of the supernatural in the world. The failure of those who would teach love and nonviolence in a world which has apostatized, which accepts no absolutes, has no standards other than utilitarian, is devoid of hope, persecutes the prophets, murders the saints, exhibits God to the people—torn, bleeding, dead.

Gandhi gained adherents, gained popularity, gained respect as he led his people to independence, for it was seen that the way of nonviolence worked in that instance. Any nationalist would have followed him there. It was because he went the full way, because he adhered to an Absolute, because he insisted that there be no hatred, that Hindu and Muslim live together in peace—it was for these things he was murdered. It was because he believed in a Revolution that went beyond the social and ended in personal regeneration, because it was as a pacifist that he has now attained to that failure that leads to ultimate glory. Truly he is one of those who has added his own sufferings to those of Christ, whose sacrifice and martyrdom will forever be offered to the Eternal Father as compensating for those things lacking in the Passion of Christ. In him we have a new intercessor with Christ; a modern Francis, a pacifist martyr.

February 1948

Peter Maurin

Dorothy returned throughout her life to writing about Peter Maurin, her mentor and co-founder of the Catholic Worker. In her obituary for Peter in The Catholic Worker *she wrote of his holiness.*

Peter was the poor man of his day. He was another St. Francis of modern times. He was used to poverty as a peasant is used to rough living, poor food, hard bed, or no bed at all, dirt, fatigue, and hard and unrespected work. He was a man with a mission, a vision, an apostolate, but he had put off from him honors, prestige, recognition. He was truly humble of heart, and loving. Never a word of detraction passed his lips and, as St. James said, the man who governs his tongue is a perfect man. He was impersonal in his love in that he loved all, saw all others around him as God saw them. In other words he saw Christ in them.

He never spoke idle words, though he was a great teacher who talked for hours on end, till late in the night and early morning. He roamed the streets and the countryside and talked to all who would listen. But when his great brain failed, he became silent. If he had been a babbler he would have been a babbler to the end. But when he could no longer think, as he himself expressed it, he remained silent.

For the last five years of his life he was this way, suffering, silent, dragging himself around, watched by us all for fear he would get lost, as he did once for three days; he was shouted at loudly by visitors as though he were deaf, talked to with condescension as one talks to a child to whom language must be simplified even to the point of absurdity. That was one of the hardest things we had to bear, we who loved him and worked with him for so long—to see others treat him as though he were simpleminded.

The fact was he had been stripped of all—he had stripped himself throughout life. He had put off the old man, to put on the new. He had done all that he could to denude himself of *the world*, and I mean the world in the evil sense, not in the sense that "God looked at it and found it good." He loved people, he saw in them what God meant them to be. He saw the world as God meant it to be, and he loved it.

He had stripped himself, but there remained work for God to do. We are to be pruned as the vine is pruned so that it can bear fruit, and this we cannot do ourselves. God did it for him. He took from him his mind, the one thing he had left, the one thing perhaps he took delight in. He could no longer think. He could no longer discuss with others, give others, in a brilliant overflow of talk, his keen analysis of what was going on in the world; he could no longer make what he called his synthesis of *cult, culture and cultivation*.

He was sick for five years. It was as though he had a stroke in his sleep. He dragged one leg after him, his face was slightly distorted, and he found it hard to speak. And he repeated, "I can no longer think." When he tried to, his face would have a strained, suffering expression.

No matter how much you expect a death, no matter how much you may regard it as a happy release, there is a gigantic sense of loss. With our love of life, we have not yet got to that point where we can say with the desert father, St. Anthony, "The spaces of this life, set over against eternity, are brief and poor."

Peter was buried in St. John's Cemetery, Queens, in a grave given us by Fr. Pierre Conway, the Dominican. Peter was another St. John, a voice crying in the wilderness, and a voice too, saying, "My little children, love one another." As the body was carried out of the church those great and triumphant words rang out, the *In Paradisum.*

> May the angels lead thee into paradise; may the martyrs receive thee at thy coming, and lead thee into the holy city of Jerusalem. May the choir of angels receive thee, and mayest thou have eternal rest with Lazarus, who once was poor.

"We need to make the kind of society," Peter had said, "where it is easier for people to be good." And because his love of God made him love his neighbor, lay down his life indeed for his brother, he wanted to cry out against the evils of the day—the State, war, usury, the degradation of man, the loss of a philosophy of work. He sang the delights of poverty (he was not talking of destitution) as a means to making a step to the land, of getting back to the dear natural things of earth and sky, of home and children. He cried out against the machine because as Pius XI had said, "raw materials went into the factory and came out ennobled and man went in and came out degraded"; and because it deprived a man of what was as important as bread, his work, his work with his hands, his ability to use all of himself, which made him a whole man and a holy man.

Yes, he talked of these material things. He knew we needed a good social order where men could grow up to their full stature and be men. And he also knew that it took men to make such a social order. He tried to form them, he tried to educate them, and God gave him poor weak materials to work with. He was as poor in the human material he had around him, as he was in material goods. We are the offscourings of all, as St. Paul said, and yet we know we have achieved great things in these brief years, and not ours is the glory. God has chosen the weak things to confound the strong, the fools of this earth to confound the wise.

Peter had been insulted and misunderstood in his life as well as loved. He had been taken for the plumber and left to sit in the basement when he had been invited for dinner and an evening of conversation. He had been thrown out of a [Knights of Columbus] meeting; one pastor who invited him to speak demanded his money back which he had sent Peter for carfare to his upstate parish, because, he said, we had sent up to him a Bowery bum and not the speaker he expected. "This then is perfect joy," Peter could say, quoting the words of St. Francis to Friar Leo, when he was teaching him where perfect joy was to be found.

He was a man of sincerity and peace, and yet one letter came to us recently, accusing him of having a holier-than-thou attitude. Yes, Peter pointed out that it was a precept that we should love God with our whole heart and soul and mind and strength, and not just a counsel, and he taught us all what it meant to be sons of God, and restored to us our sense of responsibility as lay apostles in a chaotic world. Yes, he was "holier than thou," holier than anyone we ever knew.

June 1949

SAINTS AS THEY REALLY WERE

Soon after her conversion, Dorothy began to read more about saints. She always distinguished between "saints as they really were" and the representations of pious hagiography.

At that time I did not understand that we are all "called to be saints," as St. Paul puts it. Most people nowadays, if they were asked, would say diffidently that they do not profess to be saints, indeed they do not want to be saints. And yet the saint is the holy man, the "whole man," the integrated man. We all wish to be that. But in these days of stress and strain we are not developing our spiritual capacities as we should and most of us will admit that. We want to grow in love, but we do not know how. Love is a science, a knowledge, and we lack it.

Thérèse

I began to write this article on the Feast of our Lady of Lourdes when I went to my bookshelves to find something about our Blessed Mother to read. I picked up two books, opened them for a bit and closed them both with horror and sat down with my missal instead.

In the first of the two books aforementioned, the saint-writer declares that the Blessed Mother, with lighted torches, was seen setting fire to a dance hall, where couples were carousing, and burning it to the ground with 400 people therein! The second book had a little chapter about eating: "The saints went to their meals sighing. St. Alphonsus, when sitting down, would think only of the suffering of the souls in purgatory, and with tears would beseech Our Lady to accept the mortifications he imposed upon himself during meals. Blessed [Louis] de Montfort sometimes shed tears and sobbed bitterly when sitting at table to eat. If such have been the feelings of the saints what shall we say of those of Mary? St. Jerome (in a letter to Heliodorus) said that this wonderful child only took, toward evening, the food which an angel was wont to bring her."

No wonder no one wants to be a saint. But we are called to be saints—we are the sons of God!

March 1944

This blindness of love, this folly of love—this seeing Christ in others, everywhere, and not seeing the ugly, the obvious, the dirty, the sinful—this means we do not see the faults of others, only our own. We see only Christ in them. We have eyes only for our beloved, ears for His voice.

This is what caused the saints to go to what writers like Aldous Huxley (not to speak of our own Catholics) called repulsive extremes. Perhaps hagiographers were too prone to dwell on the physical detail—one gets it too in Hemingway—in some of the writers of this present war. But it is all "to make their point," as Peter Maurin would say. The saints rose above the natural, the human, and became supernatural and superhuman in their love. Nothing was difficult to them, all was clear, shining and beautiful on the pathway of love.

What mother ever considers the ugliness of cleaning up after her baby or sick child or husband? These things are not mentioned by critics. But to the saints everyone is child and lover. Everyone is Christ.

June 1944

In all secular literature it has been so difficult to portray the good man, the saint, that a Don Quixote is made a fool and the Prince Myshkin [in Dostoevsky's *The Idiot*] an epileptic, in order to arouse the sympathy of the reader, appalled by unrelieved goodness. There are, of course, the lives of the saints, but they are too often written as though they were not in this world. We have seldom been given the saints as they really were, as they affected the lives of their times— unless it is in their own writings. But instead of that strong meat we are too generally given the pap of hagiography.

Too little has been stressed the idea that *all* are called. Too little attention has been placed on the idea of mass conversions. We have sinned against the virtue of hope. There have been in these days mass conversions to Nazism, fascism, and communism. Where are our saints to call the masses to God? Personalists first, we must put the question to ourselves. Communitarians, we will find Christ in our brothers.

May 1948, *On Pilgrimage*

As a convert, I never expected much of the bishops. In all history popes and bishops and Father Abbots seem to have been blind and power loving and greedy. I never expected leadership from them. It is the saints that keep appearing all thru history who keep things going. What I do expect is the bread of life and down thru the ages there is that continuity. Living where we do there certainly is no intellectual acceptance of the Church, only blind faith. I mean among the poor.

The gospel is hard. Loving your enemies, and the worst are of our own household, is hard.

To Gordon Zahn, October 29, 1968,
All the Way to Heaven

SAINTS TO CHANGE THE SOCIAL ORDER

In her youth, Dorothy had intuited the need for "saints to change the social order." In later years she would extol the example of the "saint-revolutionist," a figure depicted in the novels of Ignazio Silone and others outside the church.

Called to Be Saints

Naturally speaking, people are filled with repulsion at the idea of holiness. We have so many sad examples of Pecksniffs in our midst. But now we are filled with encouragement these days to find that it is not only the *Catholic Worker* but writers like Ignazio Silone, Aldous Huxley, and Arthur Koestler who are also crying aloud for a synthesis—the saint-revolutionist who would impel others to holiness by his example. And recognizing the difficulty of the aim, Silone has drawn pictures of touching fellowship with the lowly, the revolutionist living in voluntary poverty, in hunger and cold, in the stable, and depending on "personalist action" to move the world. *Bread and Wine* and *The Seed Beneath the Snow* are filled with this message.

After the last war, everyone was talking about the lost generation. After this war, thank God, they are talking more about *saints*. A few years ago there was a book review by W. H. Auden in the *New York Times* about Greek and Christian tragedy and *Moby Dick* as an allegorical novel. In that review it is pointed out that unlike Greek tragedy, where one's fate is written, where it is only up to the hero to play the heroic part, the Christian has a *choice*, and each and every lowly Christian is forced to make that choice. According to Auden,

> There is the possibility of each becoming exceptional and good; this ultimate possibility for hero and

chorus alike is stated in Father Mapple's sermon, and it is to become a saint, i.e., the individual through his own free will surrenders his will to the will of God. In this surrender he does not become the ventriloquist's doll, for the God who acts through him can only do so by his consent; there always remain two wills, and the saint therefore never ceases to be tempted to obey his own desires.

The saint does not ask to become one, he is called to become one and assents to the call. The outward sign that Ahab is so called is the suffering which is suddenly intruded into his life. He is called to give up hunting whales—"the normal, cannibalistic life of this world."

Archbishop Robichaud, in his book *Holiness for All*, emphasizes the fact that the choice is not between good and evil for Christians—that it is not in this way that one proves his love. The very fact of baptism, of becoming the son of God, presupposes development as children of God. C. S. Lewis points out that the child in the mother's womb would perhaps refuse to be born if given the choice, but it does not have that choice. It has to be born. The egg has to develop into the chicken with wings. Otherwise it becomes a rotten egg. It is not between good and evil, we repeat, that the choice lies, but between good and better. In other words, we must give up over and over again even the good things of this world to choose God. Mortal sin is a turning from God and a turning to created things—created things that are good.

It is so tremendous an idea that it is hard for people to see its implications. Our whole literature, our culture, is built on ethics, the choice between good and evil. The drama of the ages is on this theme. We are still living in the Old Testament, with commandments as to the natural law. We have not begun to live as good Jews, let alone as good Christians. We do not tithe ourselves; there is no year of Jubilee; we do not keep the Sabbath; we have lost the concept of hospitality. It is dog eat dog. We are all hunting whales. We devour each other in love and in hate; we are cannibals.

May 1948, *On Pilgrimage*

St. Benedict Joseph Labré (d. 1793) was a French pilgrim who embraced poverty, living on alms, and visiting shrines. His outward appearance attracted scorn. Yet following his death in Rome, he was quickly acclaimed as a saint. Dorothy proposed a column for the paper to be written by "Ben Joe Labray," a modern-day saint in the guise of a homeless tramp.

Our readers who have been with us for some years are well acquainted with the articles written by Ben Joe Labray, our present-day working-class saint. That character was born back in 1938 in an idle moment of waiting, specifically when Margaret Bigham and I were sitting down by the docks in New York waiting for a seaman fellow-worker to come off ship after a long South American trip. There was a copy of Sir Roger de Coverley in the car, and in starting to read about this composite character, whose articles were written by a number of men, I thought of a good idea for a series. Why not get a number of our fellow-workers to write articles which would show in some small way a new character in history, a new kind of saint for our times, the kind of saint we need, the saint-revolutionist who would not only use the spiritual weapons of prayer, poverty, and penance, but would try to begin, here and now, that kind of a social order which would indicate his sincere belief in the doctrine of brotherhood.

He would be a character half real, half imagined. He would be a saint of the poor, one of the lumpen proletariat who recognized not only the misery of his state, but the sin it led to. And I remembered St. Benedict Joseph Labré, who was a bum, who reacted against the effete delicacy of his time when men wore ruffles and laces and powder and curls, by going unwashed, in rags; who rebelled against the luxury and wealth and hoggishness of his time by asking nothing for himself (like our own Peter Maurin), who did penance for the world and died in a gutter. And in remembering him, I decided to use his name, changed somewhat, so I signed the articles which began and continued for some years, by the name of Ben Joe Labray.

I wrote the first and a few of the others. They continued until a priest in Brooklyn, whose church is named after our good saint, objected, feeling that we were casting dishonor on his patron. I wonder if his parishioners appreciated St. Ben Joe. I wonder if they would have sat next to him, in his filth and vermin, in these days when dirt and sin are synonymous in people's minds and unless you have hot and cold running water, flush toilets, daily baths, and other plumbing appurtenances, you are either slovenly poor white trash, demented, a medievalist, a loafer with no self-respect, or a machine smasher.

October 1946

We have been living for fourteen years in a community in Mott Street. Every night as we said compline, we said, "Visit O Lord this community!" And we meant the street, the neighborhood, the two parishes we lived between, the group where we felt ourselves at home, as once we felt ourselves at home in our families, "felt ourselves approved, affirmed, in our functional independence and responsibility." . . .

Here, within this great city of nine million people, we must, in this neighborhood, on this street, in this parish, regain a sense of community which is the basis for peace in the world. It is only so we can oppose the State and the present ever-spreading war. We are not represented by our so-called representatives. (The State, according to Martin Buber, is an institution in which a virtually unorganized mass allows its affairs to be conducted by "representation.")

Our representatives are the saints, the thinkers, uniting us in a community of interest, in a human relationship in this world and the next. And we have to work hard in this world, to begin our heaven now, to make a heaven for others (it has been called Utopia), because this is the teaching of the saints.

All the way to heaven is heaven, because Christ said, I am the Way. St. Catherine of Siena said this. We are to be Christ to each other, and see Christ in each other, and so we will love one another. "And for these there is no law," in the legal worldly sense, but only "the liberty of Christ." This is what we mean by our philosophical anarchism.

Our representative leaders, thinkers, and strugglers are such men as St. Vincent de Paul, St. Francis, Gandhi, Tolstoy, and such writers as Baron von Hügel and Dr. Martin Buber, two thinkers whose books I am reading right now.

October 1950

[Charles] Péguy said that the race of heroes and the race of saints stand in contradiction, the contradiction of the eternal and the temporal. He was writing of Joan of Arc and he said that the two races meet in her, which meet nowhere else. We would say they met also in Gandhi.

With the bishops of the United States pointing out that the greatest danger of our age is secularism, it would seem that it is a time when we must beg God to raise up for our time men in whom saint and hero meet to solve the problems of the day. And not by war!

January 1953

This is the month when we pray for the dead and read over again *The Dream of Gerontius*, and the teaching of St. Catherine of Genoa on Purgatory, who said that next to Heaven, that was the happiest place one could be because one is *sure* and secure. If the pains of separation are the most we have to bear, and they will be proportionate to our love, there must be great joy there. These are matters of faith, and a mystery.

Here and there in my missal, my little office, lay breviary, *Imitation*, I have lists, some of the dead, and some of the living, and when I remember the dead at Mass I always add, "all those listed in my prayer books." Eternal rest grant unto them, O Lord, and let perpetual light shine upon them.

There are lists of saints in the Mass, and time out for us to remember the living and the dead. And my dead include martyrs of the labor movement, Harlan County miners, Memorial Day massacre victims, the five little children killed in Birmingham, and all those tortured and lynched by all our fellow human beings who give themselves over to those black forces of evil—of cruelty and hatred and lust for murder, which rise within them and take possession of them. Oh, God, you must—you will—wipe away all tears from their eyes, you must make up to them for all the agony they have endured, which their families have endured.

November 1964

PUTTING ON CHRIST

The call to holiness was rooted in our very baptismal vows, and it was an ongoing call throughout our lives: "to put off the old man and put on Christ."

St. Paul said to put off the old man and put on Christ. Poverty is no good supernaturally if it is a pagan poverty for the sake of the freedom involved, though that is good, naturally speaking. Poverty is good, because we share the poverty of others, we know them and so love them more. Also, by embracing poverty we can give away to others. If we eat less, others can have more. If we pay less rent, we can pay the rent of a dispossessed family. If we go with old clothes, we can clothe others. We can perform the corporal works of mercy by embracing poverty.

If we embrace poverty, we put on Christ. If we put off the world, if we put the world out of our hearts, there is room for Christ within.

Solitude is no good unless it is "to be still and see that I am God." God said, "It is not good for man to live alone." But occasionally Jesus calls and says, "Let us go apart and rest awhile." By this practice of solitude, one can learn to put the world out, to put on Christ.

One has to practice loving one's neighbor, seeing Christ in one's neighbor.

Christ offered His death for the sins of the world. So we offer our voluntary and involuntary pains and sufferings for the sins of the world, my own and others. Accepting gladly, joyously, by no matter who inflicted. To pray with outstretched arms, to keep vigil when the whole body is tortured with the desire for sleep, to scourge oneself, to fast.

A German woman doctor who spent a year in a concentration camp for refusing to sterilize epileptics said that one form of torture inflicted was to turn blinding light into the cells so that the women could not sleep. This is to be keeping vigil with Christ. To keep vigil voluntarily is to be sharing this pain of the world, this agony of the Mystical Body. Insomnia may be keeping vigil.

To train oneself for the race, to train oneself to a joyful acceptance, a loving acceptance. To love one's enemies.

"Father, forgive them for they know not what they do."

Jesus said to a fellow-sufferer, who accepted his pains, "This day shalt thou be with Me in Paradise."

St. Peter said, not long after the death of Jesus, "And now brothers, comrades, I know that you acted in ignorance, as did also your rulers. Repent then and be converted." What hope! What optimism! What foolishness. It is the folly of the cross. Can a Hitler be converted and live? God, I believe, help thou mine unbelief. Let me see Christ in him. Take away my heart of stone, and give me a heart of flesh. Teach me to love.

Help me, Jesus of Nazareth, King of the Jews, have mercy on me, a sinner. Help me to make a tiny beginning at building up that great and mighty force of love which will overcome Fear.

How mighty is that force. How terrible and beautiful a thing it is to fall into the hands of a living God. Teach us, God, Holy and Mighty one, what Love is!

January 1944

Failures. It is these things that overwhelm one. Physical sickness like epilepsy, senility, insanity, drug cases, alcoholics; and just the plain, ordinary poor who can't get along, can't find a place to live, who need clothes, shelter, food, jobs, care, and most of all love—these are the daily encounters.

So it is wonderful that this retreat comes in the middle of summer, when one can stop and think in his heart about these things. I have made this retreat eight times, and always there is something new, always there is something to learn about how to progress in the love of God and one's neighbor. How can we ever give up thinking and longing for love, talking of it, preparing ourselves for it, reading of it, studying about it? It is really a great faith in love that never dies. We hope against hope, as Abraham did in the promise, and we know with something that bears witness in us that this love is true, and that the promise is there.

I am speaking of heavenly things, but heaven and earth are linked together as the body and soul are linked together. We begin to live again each morning. We rise from the dead, the sun rises, spring comes around—there is always that cycle of birth and growth and death, and then resurrection. And the great study of how truly to become the sons of God, to be made like God, to participate in the life of God—this is the study of the retreat. It is a painful study, and one can make it over and over again, and always we need to straighten our course, adjust ourselves to this upside-down way of looking at things, which is the Christian way and which seems so often to be not common sense, not natural. It is breathing rarefied air; one must get used to this air of the mountains, so clear, cold, sharp, and fresh. It is like wine, and we have prayed to Mary and said, "We have no wine," and she has given us wine, the body and blood of her Son, the life of her Son, the love of her Son.

My whole life so far, my whole experience has been that our failure has been not to love enough. This conviction brought me to a rejection of the radical movement after my early membership in the Socialist Party, the Industrial Workers of the World, and the Communist affiliates I worked with. "Youth demands the heroic," as Claudel said, so the work of these militant minorities had appealed to me. One could not read such books as Sinclair's *The Jungle* and not want to do something, join with someone to do something about it. And who else was doing anything? Employers, landlords, political bosses, all professed Christians, were corrupt and rotten to the core, I felt. What was there to love in them? Certainly it seemed madness to think of reforming them, converting them. Such an Augean stable was beyond cleaning up; it needed flushing out. So I reasoned. Youth certainly is always looking for a "strong conflict."

It was not that I was ever disillusioned. My conviction that there was a work to be done never wavered. Things did not need to be as bad as they were. There was a possibility of change.

Certainly, too, there was always an inward conviction that we were but dust. Alone by ourselves, we could do nothing. Probably all my early religiousness as a child was still with me, and that religiousness included a conviction of sin, of the depravity that was in us all. The argument of conscience was always there. I was "bad" or I was "good." I was bad when I hated and quarreled with my brothers and sisters, when I stole from a neighbor's garden, when I was impure (and I felt that "dark fascination" of sex, of the physical forces in my own body, very early).

This reminds me of St. Augustine's *Confessions* and his story of childhood wickedness, stealing for the sake of stealing, deliberately giving way to evil, to the dark forces within one. *The Turn of the Screw* is a story of childish evil. Jesus Christ knew what was in man. I was not baptized until I was twelve, but I had a conscience. I knew what was in man too. But I had too a tremendous faith in man as a temple of the Holy Ghost, made [in] the image and likeness of God, a little less than the angels. Truly I did not want to know good and evil. I wanted to know, to believe only the good. I wanted to believe that man could right wrongs, could tilt the lance, could love and espouse the cause of his brother because "an injury to one was an injury to all." I never liked the appeal to enlightened self-interest. I wanted to love my fellows; I loved the poor with compassion. I could not be happy unless I shared poverty, lived as they did, suffered as they did.

Well, now at fifty, I cannot say that I have been disillusioned. But I cannot say either that I yet share the poverty and the suffering of the poor. No matter how much I may live in a slum, I can never be poor as the mother of three, six, ten children is poor (or rich either). I can never give up enough. I have always to struggle against self. I am not disillusioned with myself either. I know my talents and abilities as well as failures. But I have done woefully little. I am fifty, and more than half of my adult life is past. Who knows how much time is left after fifty? Newman says the tragedy is never to have begun.

July–August 1948

We have not yet begun to know what men are capable of in the spiritual order, what growth, what joy! Father Henri de Lubac, S.J., wrote recently, "It is not the proper duty of Christianity to form leaders—that is, builders of the temporal, though a legion of Christian leaders is infinitely desirable. Christianity must generate saints—that is, witnesses to the eternal. The efficacy of the saint is not that of the leader. The saint does not have to bring about great temporal achievements; he is one who succeeds in giving us at least a glimpse of eternity despite the thick opacity of time."

We are all called to be saints, St. Paul says, and we might as well get over our bourgeois fear of the name. We might also get used to recognizing the fact that there is some of the saint in all of us. Inasmuch as we are growing, putting off the old man and putting on Christ, there is some of the saint, the holy, the divine right there. . . .

We are called to be saints. Sometimes we don't see them around us, sometimes their sanctity is obscured by the human, but they are there nonetheless.

The Third Hour, 1949, *Selected Writings*

As for saints, in the old translation of Scripture St. Paul greeted people in his letters as "called to be saints." And wrote also that we should put off "the old man" and "put on Christ." "Be ye therefore holy." In other words "whole men," developing all our faculties—spiritual, mental, and physical. When I think how men have walked on the moon—their courage, their faith—how highly developed their mental and physical capacities, I feel we are woefully undeveloped spiritually.

And yet, there is always some aspect of saintliness in the folks around the CW. So many young people getting down to the essentials of life, pruning away the non-essentials, learning to meditate, to contemplate. They are on a quest, a search for wholeness, holiness.

The Quakers have a saying, "There is that which is of God in every man." In other words, seeing Christ in each other, as He told us to do. "Whatever you did for one of my least brethren, you have done for me." We so often apply these words to the works of mercy—feeding, clothing and sheltering others—but those in trouble who come to the Catholic Worker do the same for us and each other. The "little" saints like Hans who taught everyone to bake bread, and Mike who was so knowledgeable about furnaces and water heaters, and Tom Likely who set tables, cut bread, mixed powdered milk, kept kettles hot, served up tea and coffee to the disconsolate; and now, our latest "departed" friend, Bob Stewart, who chauffeured for us so many years, so uncomplaining in those last months of emphysema.

And all those other quiet men who drop by "off the road" who help in so many little ways. If I'm not careful I'll sound like the Irish who see sanctity everywhere. What a variety of people "called to be saints," crotchety, giddy, cranky ones, bibulous ones. It is no mean ambition—to aspire to holiness—to wholeness.

I always liked to read about saints. In all bad times of luxury and corruption in the Church, there was always a St. Francis, a St. Anthony, a St. Benedict, a Vincent de Paul, a Teresa and a Thérèse on the scene to enliven history. Georges Bernanos, who wrote *The Diary of a Country Priest*, wrote also that famous line: "There is only one sadness, not to be a saint."

So let us all, with St. Paul, "rejoice in the Lord always," remembering Christ's beatitudes, and call on the Name of the Lord—recalling too St. Bernard's words—"Jesus is honey in the mouth, music to the ear, and shout of gladness in the heart," because Christ, our Incarnate God, is present in His Name as in His Word, even as He was in the cloud which went before the Israelites.

When I write like this, it is for myself, too, that I write, because this last month, after returning from my pilgrimage, my heart was heavy with the sufferings of little babies undergoing major operations that is hardest for me to bear.

So let us pray for each other and "rejoice" because we share in some way the sufferings of others, and in some mysterious way lighten our own as we pray that the sufferings of others be lightened.

June 1974

5

The Little Way

Dorothy Day is rightly remembered as a courageous activist, the leader of a lay Catholic movement, the editor of a newspaper, who was frequently arrested for the cause of peace and justice. In that light it may be curious to discover her devotion to St. Thérèse of Lisieux, a Carmelite nun who died in 1897 at the age of twenty-four in a small convent in Normandy. At first glance, these two women, the activist and the contemplative, would appear to have little in common.

Dorothy's devotion to the Little Flower, as St. Thérèse is popularly known, is all the more striking in light of her initial reaction. Upon first reading Thérèse's autobiography, soon after her conversion, she found it "colorless, monotonous, too small in fact for my notice." In short: "pious pap." It took many years for her to change her mind. "I much preferred to read about spectacular saints who were impossible to imitate," she wrote. And yet she would come to see in Thérèse not only a great saint but one with a message of special relevance for our times.

Thérèse had indicated a path to holiness that lay in performing all our daily tasks and duties in a spirit of love and in the presence of God. She called this path the Little Way. From Thérèse, Dorothy learned that each sacrifice endured in love, each work of mercy, might increase the balance of love in the world. She extended this principle to the social sphere. Each protest or witness for peace—

though apparently foolish and ineffective, no more than a pebble in a pond—might send forth ripples that could transform the world.

Dorothy spent some years in the early 1950s writing a biography of Thérèse. Her main point, as she described it to a friend, was "to make people realize their personal responsibility, how everything they do matters." Although many books had been written about St. Thérèse, she noted, "The social implications of her teachings are yet to be written. The significance of our smallest acts! The significance of the little things we leave undone! The protests we do not take, we who are living in the world!"

In the end, neither she nor her publisher was entirely satisfied with her book. But the principles of Thérèse's "Little Way" continued to permeate all of Dorothy's writings. They are demonstrated in her conviction that the arena of holiness lies in the daily exercise of charity, forgiveness, and the choice to curb our impulse to anger and resentment—occasions that arose every day in a house of hospitality. It was this practice in all the ordinary events and encounters of her life that equipped Dorothy for the extraordinary and heroic actions she performed on a wider scale.

ENCOUNTERING THÉRÈSE

The first time Dorothy heard about St. Thérèse was from a woman she met in the maternity ward, where she had just given birth to her daughter. Learning that Dorothy planned to name her daughter Tamar Teresa, this young mother offered her a pin of the Little Flower. Dorothy was still some months from becoming a Catholic, and she "shied away from this evidence of superstition and charm-wearing." The next time was from her confessor.

The next time I heard of St. Thérèse of Lisieux was in 1928, a year after I had been baptized a Catholic. I was thirty years old. I had read the New Testament, the *Imitation of Christ*, Saint Augustine, and had dipped into the writings of the saints William James had introduced me to. I had a Daily Missal, too, which presented a little biography of the saint of the day, commemorated in the Mass. I still knew nothing of modern saints. Perhaps, I thought, the days of saints had passed. . . .

My confessor at the time was Fr. Zachary, an Augustinian Father of the Assumption, stationed at the Church of Our Lady of Guadalupe on West Fourteenth Street. He was preparing me for Confirmation, giving me a weekly evening of instruction.

One day Father Zachary said to me, "Here is a book that will do you good." He had already given me Challoner's *Meditations* and the Saint Andrew Missal. The book he now handed me was *The Little White Flower: The Story of a Soul,* an unbound book which had a tan cover with a not-too-attractive picture of a young nun with a sweet, insipid face, holding a crucifix and a huge bouquet of roses. I was by now familiar with the statues of this little sister which were to be seen in every Church. They always called her little, although it is said she was very tall, and completely emaciated when the last photographs of her were taken. She had a proud face, however, and her habit and cloak concealed how thin she was. She was very young and her writing seemed to be me like a schoolgirl. I wasn't looking for anything so simple and felt slightly aggrieved at Father Zachary. Men, even priests, were very insulting to women, I thought, handing out what they thought suited their intelligence—in other words, pious pap.

I dutifully read *The Story of a Soul* and am ashamed to confess that I found it colorless, monotonous, too small in fact for my notice. What kind of a saint was this who felt that she had to practice heroic charity in eating what was put in front of her, in taking medicine, enduring cold and heat, restraint, enduring the company of mediocre souls, in following the strict regime of the Carmelite nuns which she had joined at the age of fifteen? A splash of dirty water from the careless washing of a nun next to her was mentioned as a "mortification," when the very root of the word meant death. And I was reading in my Daily Missal of saints stretched on the rack, burnt by flames, starving themselves in the desert, and so on.

Joan of Arc leading an army fitted more into my concept of a saint, familiar as I was with the history of labor, with its martyrs in the service of their brothers. "Love of brothers is to lay down one's life on the barricades, in revolt against the hunger and injustice in the world," I told Father Zachary, trying to convert him to my point of view. Living as we were in a time of world revolution, when, as I felt, the people of the world were rising to make a better world for themselves, I wondered what this new saint had to offer. . . .

It took me a longer time to realize the unique position of Thérèse of Lisieux in the Church today.

Thérèse

In the conclusion to her book about St. Thérèse, Dorothy summed up the meaning of her holiness and the secret of her appeal.

Thérèse Martin died on September 30, 1897. Only seventeen years later, when those who had been born in the same year with her were just forty-one years of age, the fame of her sanctity had so spread among the people that her cause was introduced at Rome. She was beatified on April 29, 1923, and canonized on May 17, 1925, an unusually rapid process for the Church in modern times.

So many books have been written about St. Thérèse, books of all kinds, too, so why, I ask myself again, have I written one more? There are popular lives, popular lives written for children, travelogue lives, following her footsteps, lives for the extrovert, the introvert, the contemplative, the activist, the scholar, and the theologian.

Yet it was the "worker," the common man, who first spread her fame by word of mouth. It was the masses who first proclaimed her a saint. It was the "people."

What was there about her to make such an appeal? Perhaps because she was so much like the rest of us in her ordinariness. In her lifetime, there are no miracles recounted; she was just good, good as the bread which the Normans bake in huge loaves. Good as the pale cider which takes the place of the wine of the rest of France, since Normandy is an apple country. "Small beer," one might say. She compares to the great saints as cider compares with wine, others might complain. But it is the world itself which has canonized her. It is the common people who have taken her to their hearts. And now the theologians are writing endlessly to explain how big she was, and not little, how mature and strong she was, not child-like and dependent. They are tired of hearing people couple her name with Teresa of Avila, whom they call the "Great Teresa" as distinguished from the "Little Thérèse."

What did she do? She practiced the presence of God and she did all things—all the little things that make up our daily life and contact with others—for His honor and glory. She did not need much time to expound what she herself called her "little way." She wrote her story, and God did the rest. God and the people. God chose for the people to clamor for her canonization.

What stands out in her life? Her holiness, of course, and the holiness of her entire family. That is not an ordinary thing in this day of post-war materialism, delinquency, and all those other words which indicate how dissatisfied the West is with its economy of abundance while the East sits like Lazarus at the gate of Dives.

With governments becoming stronger and more central-ized, the common man feels his ineffectiveness. When the whole world seems given over to preparedness for war and the show of force, the message of Thérèse is quite a different one.

She speaks to our condition. Is the atom a little thing? And yet what havoc it has wrought. Is her little way a small contribution to the life of the spirit? It has all the power of the spirit of Christianity behind it. It is an explosive force that can transform our lives and the life of the world, once put into effect. In the homily he gave after the Gospel at the Mass of her canonization, Pope Pius XI said: "If the way of spiritual childhood became general, who does not see how easily would be realized the reformation of human society. . . ."

The seeds of this teaching are being spread, being broad-cast, to be watered by our blood perhaps, but with a promise of a harvest. God will give the increase. At a time when there are such grave fears because of the radioactive particles that are sprinkled over the world by the hydrogen bomb tests, and the question is asked, what effect they are going to have on the physical life of the universe. One can state that this saint, of this day, is releasing a force, a spiritual force upon the world, to counteract that fear and that disaster. We know that one impulse of grace is of infinitely more power than a cobalt bomb. Thérèse has said, "All is grace."

She declared, "I will spend my heaven doing good upon earth." "I will raise up a mighty host of little saints." "My mission is to make God beloved, to make Love loved."

And one can only remember the story of Abraham and how he asked, "Wilt Thou destroy the just with the wicked? If there be fifty just men in the city, they shall perish with all? And wilt Thou not spare that place for the sake of the fifty just, if they be therein? Far be it from Thee to do this thing and to slay the just with the wicked and for the just to be in like case as the wicked? This is not beseeming Thee: Thou, who judgest all the earth, wilt not make this judgment."

The mystery of suffering has a different aspect under the New Covenant, since Christ died on the Cross and took on Himself men's sins. Now St. Paul teaches that we can fill up the sufferings of Christ, that we must share in the sufferings of the world to lessen them, to show our love for our brothers. But God does not change, so we can trust with Abraham that for even ten just men, He will not destroy the city. We can look with faith and hope to that *mighty army of little ones* that St. Thérèse has promised us and which is present now among us.

Thérèse

LESSONS IN THE LITTLE WAY

It takes heroic virtue to practice patience in little things, things which seem little to others but which afflict one with unrest and misery. Patience with each other and with each other's bickering. We can even offer up, however, our own lack of peace, our own worry. Since I offered all my distractions, turmoil, and unrest I felt at things going askew a few weeks ago, my petty fretting over this one and that one, I have felt much better and able to cope with everything.

August 7, 1937, *The Duty of Delight*

Out in the backyard there is a little garden with sunflowers, marigolds, petunias, and ice plant. Out in front there is one tree.

How little it all is, as obscure as the life of the Blessed Mother and as "little" as the life and sufferings of the Little Flower! . . .

The only answer to this mystery of suffering is this. Every soul seeks happiness either in creatures (where it cannot be satisfied in the long run) or in God. God made us for Himself.

We must die to the natural to achieve the supernatural, a slow death or a quick one. It is universal. "Unless the grain of wheat fall into the ground and die, itself remaineth alone, but if it die, it beareth much fruit." All must die; it is a universal law, very hard for us to realize.

If this mind or this flesh is an obstacle, we will suffer the more when this tremendous Lover tries to tear from us all veils which separate us. Some suffering is more visible, some hidden. If we long for beauty, the more our faith is tried, as though by fire, by ugliness. The more we long for love, the more all human love will be pruned, and the more we will see the venom of hatred about us. It is a pruning, a cutting away of love so that it will grow strong and bear much fruit. The more we long for power, the more we will destroy and tear down until we recognize our own weakness.

But still, suffering is a mystery as well as a penalty which we pay for others as well as for ourselves. I feel presumptuous in writing of so high and lofty a thing. It is because I am not now suffering that I can write, but it is also because I have suffered in the past that I can write.

I write to comfort others as I have been comforted. The word *comfort* too means to be strong together, to have fortitude together. There is the reminder of community. Once when I suffered and sat in church in a misery while waves and billows passed over me, I suddenly thought, with exultation, "I am sharing suffering," and it was immediately lightened. But usually it is as the Little Flower said: "Let us suffer if need be with bitterness and without courage. Jesus truly suffered with sadness. Without sadness, would the soul suffer? And we would suffer generously, grandly; what an illusion!"

Compassion—it is a word meaning "to suffer with." If we all carry a little of the burden, it will be lightened. If we share in the suffering of the world, then some will not have to endure so heavy an affliction. It evens out. What you do here in New York, in Harrisburg, helps those in China, India, South Africa, Europe, [and] Russia, as well as in the oasis where you are. You may think you are alone. But we are members one of another. We are children of God together.

October 1948, *On Pilgrimage*

The Little Flower said: "I should not be happy in heaven if I was not able to provide little pleasures on earth for those I love. . . . I shall spend my heaven doing good upon earth." I like these quotations. Either the Little Flower is looked upon (perhaps because of her nickname) with sentimentality, or, as one gets to know her better, with dread. On that frail battleground of her flesh were fought the wars of today. When she died her bones were piercing her body and she died in an agony of both flesh and spirit. She was tempted against faith and said that for the last years of her life she forced herself to believe with her indomitable will while a mocking voice cried in her ears that there was neither heaven nor hell, and she was flinging away her life for nothing. To her God was a consuming flame. "It is a terrible thing to fall into the hands of the living God," St. Peter said with exultation. We have to pay a great and terrible price but "underneath are the everlasting arms." Thank God for the saints whose feast days come around and remind us that we too are called to be saints.

October 1949

It is a penance to work, to give oneself to others, to endure the pinpricks of community living. One would certainly say on many occasions: Give me a good thorough frank, outgoing war, rather than the sneak attacks, stabs in the back, sparring, detracting, defaming, hand-to-hand jockeying for position that goes on in offices and "good works" of all kinds, another and miserably petty kind of war. St. Paul said that he "died daily." This too is penance to be taken cheerfully, joyfully, with the hope that our own faith and joy I believe will strengthen all the others in jail.

Let us rejoice in our own petty suffering and thank God we have a little penance to offer, in this holy season. "An injury to one is an injury to all," the Industrial Workers of the World proclaimed. So an act of love, a voluntary taking on oneself of some of the pain of the world, increases the courage and love and hope of all.

February 1969

THE SOCIAL DIMENSION

I'd like to finish my new book on St. Thérèse, a short affair (a woman's book). The main point of it being to make people realize their personal responsibility, how everything they do matters. Most young people have such a sense of futility these days—they are paralyzed.

To Ammon Hennacy, February 1952,
All the Way to Heaven

Do What Comes to Hand

Today we are not content with little achievements, with small beginnings. We should look to St. Thérèse, the Little Flower, to walk her little way of love. We should look to St. Teresa of Avila, who was not content to be like those people who proceeded with the pace of hens about God's business, but like those people who on their own account were greatly daring in what they wished to do for God. It is we ourselves that we have to think about, no one else. That is the way the saints worked. They paid attention to what they were doing, and if others were attracted to them by their enterprise, why, well and good. But they looked to themselves first of all.

Do what comes to hand. Whatsoever thy hand finds to do, do it with all thy might. After all, God is with us. It shows too much conceit to trust in ourselves, to be discouraged at what we ourselves can accomplish. It is lacking in faith in God to be discouraged. After all, we are going to proceed with His help. We offer Him what we are going to do. If He wishes it to prosper, it will. We must depend solely on Him. Work as though everything depended on ourselves, and pray as though everything depended on God, as St. Ignatius says. . . .

I suppose it is a grace not to be able to have time or derive satisfaction in the work we are doing. In what time I have, my impulse is to self-criticism and examination of conscience and I am constantly humiliated at my own imperfections and at my halting progress. Perhaps I deceive myself here, too, and excuse my lack of recollection. But I do know how small I am and how little I can do and I beg You, Lord, to help me, for I cannot help myself.

House of Hospitality

Throwing Our Pebble

What we would like to do is change the world—make it a little simpler for people to feed, clothe, and shelter themselves as God intended them to do. And to a certain extent, by fighting for better conditions, by crying out unceasingly for the rights of the workers, of the poor, of the destitute, we can to a certain extent change the world; we can work for the oasis, the little cell of joy and peace in a harried world. We can throw our pebble in the pond and be confident that its ever-widening circle will reach around the world.

We repeat, there is nothing that we can do but love, and dear God—please enlarge our hearts to love each other, to love our neighbor, to love our enemy as well as our friend.

June 1946

The Mystery of Suffering

How to draw a picture of the strength of love! It seems at times that we need a blind faith to believe in it at all. There is so much failure all about us. It is so hard to reconcile oneself to such suffering, such long, enduring suffering of body and soul, that the only thing one can do is to stand by and save the dying ones who have given up hope of reaching out for beauty, joy, ease, and pleasure in this life. For all their reaching, they got little of it. To see these things in the light of faith, God's mercy, God's justice! His devouring love! I read one story of the death of the Little Flower, and her death was just as harrowing in its suffering as that of Mary's Katie. Her flesh was a mass of sores; her bones protruded through her skin; she was a living skeleton, a victim of love. We have not such compassion, nor ever will have. What we do is so little.

The stink of the world's injustice and the world's indifference is all around us. . . .

October 1948, *On Pilgrimage*

Inventory

This last year, at St. Joseph's House of Hospitality, we gave out, roughly speaking and underestimating it at that, 460,000 meals. Also 18,250 nights' lodging. This is what the world sees and if we wished to impress the world we would multiply this by eighteen years, and the figures would be truly impressive.

But suppose a mother should say, in a plea for sympathy, "I've put one thousand and ninety-five meals on the table this last year. I've washed fifty thousand plates."

It is easy to see how foolish it is to look at things in this light, in this big way. I am sure that God is not counting the meals. He is looking at Tony Aratari, Joe Monroe, Ray Taylor, turning off their alarm clocks at five every morning to go downstairs to start the coffee, cut the bread. They get no credit for being noble. They have no realization of dying to themselves, of giving up their lives. They are more often than not abused by friends and relatives for not getting jobs, using their education, "supporting themselves," instead of living on charity. "This then is perfect joy," as St. Francis would say.

We all wish for recognition of one kind or another. But it is mass action people think of these days. They lose sight of the sacrament of the present moment—of the little way.

Like Lord Jim, in Conrad's story, We are all waiting for great opportunities to show heroism, letting countless opportunities go by to enlarge our hearts, increase our faith, and show our love for our fellows, and so for Him. As St. Paul says, it is by little and by little we are saved—or that we fall. We are living in this world and must make choices now, choices which may mean the sacrifice of our lives, in the future, but for now our goods, our reputations even. Our work is called futile, our stand of little worth or significance, having no influence, winning no converts, ineffective if not a form of treason. Or it is termed defeatism, appeasement, escapism.

What a paradox it is, this natural life and this supernatural life. We must give up our lives to gain them; we must die to live; we must be pruned to bear fruit. Ah yes, when we are being called appeasers, defeatists, we are being deprived of our dearest goods, our reputation, honor, the esteem of men—and we are truly on the way to becoming the despised of the earth. We are beginning perhaps to be truly poor.

We are trying to spread the gospel of peace, to persuade others, to extend the peace movement, to build up a mighty army of conscientious objectors. And in doing this we are accounted fools, and it is the folly of the Cross in the eyes of an unbelieving world.

Martyrdom is not gallantly standing before a firing squad. Usually it is the losing of a job because of not taking a loyalty oath, or buying a war bond, or paying a tax. Martyrdom is small, hidden, misunderstood. Or if it is a bloody martyrdom, it is the cry in the dark, the terror, the shame, the loneliness, nobody to hear, nobody to suffer with, let alone to save. Oh, the loneliness of all of us in these days, in all the great moments of our lives, this dying which we do, by little and by little, over a short space of time or over the years. One day is as a thousand in these crises. A week in jail is as a year.

But we repeat that we do see results from our personal experiences and we proclaim our faith. Christ has died for us. Adam and Eve fell, and as Julian of Norwich wrote, the worst has already happened and been repaired. Christ continues to die in His martyrs all over the world, in His Mystical Body and it is this dying, not the killing in wars, which will save the world today.

Do we see results, do these methods succeed? Can we trust in them? Just as surely as we believe in "the little way" St. Thérèse proclaimed we believe and know that this is the only success.

January 1951

No Party Line

When we read in the papers of a captain of a freighter battling the elements and risking his life to save his ship in a ferocious sea, or the killing of a salesman in Brooklyn, or the death of a little child from beating and starvation, our hearts are torn. We have a fatalistic sense of taking part in a gigantic tragedy, a fearful adventure. Our life is charged with drama, about which we can do nothing. Our role is already written for us.

The war in Korea in which we are engaged takes on that great simplicity. We are at war because of our sins. All the suffering, the misery of the needy and the groaning of the poor, is part of the world's suffering which makes up the suffering of Christ.

Most of us try to forget and look for what we can: "eat, drink and be merry." Even the great St. Teresa was said to have remarked, as she danced during a recreation hour to the scandal of the others nuns, "One has got to do something to make life bearable."

One of the reasons I am writing a life of St. Thérèse of Lisieux, the Little Flower, is because she was determined to do something about it, even though she was imprisoned to all intents and purposes, in a small French convent in Normandy, unknown to all the world. She is the saint of the little way, the saint of the responsible.

Because she was a saint, her words were scattered like seeds profligately all over the world. Books about her are read, her autobiography has gone into many editions. But the social implications of her teachings are yet to be written. The significance of our smallest acts! The significance of the little things we leave undone! The protests we do not make, the stands we do not take, we who are living in the world!

I'm not trying to say that the Little Flower would have gone out on picket lines and spoken on Communist platforms or embraced her Protestant neighbors, if there were any in the town of Alençon. She was a product of her environment, bourgeois, middle class, the daughter of skilled workers, comfortable, frugal people who lived apart from the world with their eyes on God. She wanted everything, she said, every apostolate. And used the means at her disposal to participate in everything, to increase the sum total of the love of God in the world by every minute act, every suffering, every movement of her body and soul, done for the love of God and the love of souls. She used the spiritual weapons every one of us has at our disposal.

All this is by way of preamble for the stands we have taken, the protests we have made during the month. . . .

We are in favor of life. We are trying to work here and now for the brotherhood of man, with those minorities, those small groups of "willful men" who believe that even the few can cry out against injustice, against the man-made suffering in the world, in behalf of those who are hungry and homeless and without work, in behalf of the dying. . . .

We knelt in the library to say the rosary this noon, and some sat and Slim turned down the radio and covered his eyes while he waited for us to finish, and Catherine ceased her crossword puzzle, and Shorty and California George sat and their lips moved soundlessly. And I knelt there, and looked at their feet, at the holes in Shorty's socks, which exposed his bony ankles; and the mismatched socks and shoes on George, too long, too stylish, and ripping at the seams. They are the meek; they epitomize the poor. They do not cry out.

But we are the articulate, and we must speak and write for them. And we have no party line.

April 1952

The problems of human poverty are so vast; we see the struggle in South Africa, the war in Korea, the famine in India, China gone over to Communism, and we think how little we can do. But with a sense of the Mystical Body, the knowledge comes that we can lower or heighten the strength and love in that Body, we can work as Helen [Caldwell Day] does [in Blessed Martin de Porres House, in Memphis], among the least of God's children. Every act in that little house is an act of love, a gesture of love which reanimates and increases love and builds up this great force of love to overcome hatred and evil in the world. Poverty and precarity, self-denial and suffering, surely here is a tremendous use of the spiritual weapons, a letting loose of grace upon the world far more powerful than any atom or hydrogen bomb.

November 1952

Loaves and Fishes

When I lay in jail thinking of . . . war and peace and the problem of human freedom, of jails, drug addiction, prostitution, and the apathy of great masses of people who believe that nothing can be done—when I thought of these things I was all the more confirmed in my faith in the little way of St. Thérèse. We do the things that come to hand, we pray our prayers and beg also for an increase of faith—God will do the rest.

One of the greatest evils of the day among those outside of prison is their sense of futility. Young people say, "What good can one person do?" What is the sense of our small effort? They cannot see that we must lay one brick at a time, take one step at a time; we can be responsible only for the one action of the present moment. But we can beg for an increase of love in our hearts that will vitalize and transform all our individual actions, and know that God will take them and multiply them, as Jesus multiplied the loaves and fishes.

Loaves and Fishes

Powerlessness

I wrote the life of St. Thérèse because she exemplified the "little way." We know how powerless we are, all of us, against the power of wealth and government and industry and science. The powers of this world are overwhelming. Yet it is hoping against hope and believing, in spite of "unbelief," crying by prayer and by sacrifice, daily, small, constant sacrificing of one's own comfort and cravings—these are the things that count.

And old as I am, I see how little I have done, how little I have accomplished along these lines.

When I went to jail in the fifties, for civil disobedience—and a few of us were arrested each year for six years—I felt glad as I entered my cell that now at last I could be really poor for a time, for a day, a week, or a month, that for no matter how small a time, I was at last sharing the little misery of the poor. In a way it was true. I was stripped, prodded and searched for drugs, pushed from here to there, interminably, caged half the 24 hours like a wild beast—yes, I had just enough of it to teach me to suffer more keenly for the rest of my life over the plight of the prisoner. And not only the *grown* prisoners but the little children, in their detention homes, "youth houses," or whatever the city and state call them. And what of the refugee? The "displaced," the "relocated"?

Being in prison was dramatically to be "poor," but I soon reached out for the luxuries of something to read, the letters sent in to me, something to eat. Yes, as soon as I was permitted to go to the commissary I got me a jar of instant coffee and so could indulge myself early mornings before the cells were unlocked, with the luxury of hot water from the tap (think of it, an open toilet in the cell, and tiny washbowl).

How can I condemn the expensive drinks of the activists in the peace movement when I myself hang on to my comfort, my own addiction—"judge not."

I am convinced that prayer and austerity, prayer and self-sacrifice, prayer and fasting, prayer, vigils, and prayer and marches, are the indispensable means. . . . And love.

All these means are useless unless animated by love.

"Love your enemies." That is the hardest saying of all.

Please, Father in Heaven who made me, take away my heart of stone and give me a heart of flesh to love my enemy.

It is a terrible thought—"we love God as much as the one we love the least."

To Mike Cullen, February 1970,
All the Way to Heaven

6

THE PRACTICE OF THE
PRESENCE OF GOD

*It was always a struggle to maintain a spirit of prayer in the midst
of the noise, demands, and distractions of life in a house of hospitality. Often, Dorothy returned for inspiration to a handful of
spiritual classics. One of these was* Abandonment to Divine
Providence *by the seventeenth-century French Jesuit Jean-Pierre
de Caussade. Every moment, he taught, is given to us from God
and so bears God's will for us. Thus, when we "accept what we
cannot avoid and endure with love and resignation things which
cause us weariness and disgust," we are following the path to sanctification. He even spoke of the "sacrament of the present moment."
To live in such consciousness, he believed, was the meaning of faith.*

*The significance of the present moment was also one of the
themes of* The Practice of the Presence of God *by Brother Lawrence, a French Carmelite of the seventeenth century, who was
assigned to work in his monastery kitchen. He too, like Caussade
and also St. Thérèse, believed that by doing all one's daily tasks
and chores in the presence and love of God, ordinary life could be
transformed into a form of prayer. By this method, all our activities would be hallowed, and we could see ourselves in a state of
continuous "conversation with God."*

ON SIMPLE PRAYER

This article is taken from Dorothy's introduction to an edition of
The Practice of the Presence of God, *published by Templegate*
Press in 1974. It was reprinted in The Catholic Worker.

This book, made up of a few conversations, a few letters, has come down to us through the centuries, and is too little known. It is a classic, and carries a message, points a way. It tells of a spirituality which is within the reach of all. Most men and women have to work for a living. A philosopher once said, "Do what you are doing"—that is, pay attention to what you are doing. Brother Lawrence obviously had no books in his kitchen, to study ways of finding God. He had to find his way, obviously by prayer.

But how to pray? St. Teresa of Avila wrote many books on prayer, St. John of the Cross too, and books have been written about their books, further expounding the meaning of prayer. St. Paul told us all to search the scripture and to pray without ceasing. Both commands must have presented difficulties to Brother Lawrence, who spent his life in a kitchen or in the marketplace finding the bread and wine, meat and vegetables for a community. Certainly there was little time for the delightful occupation of *reading* about prayer.

I am sure the disciples of Jesus did little reading, fishermen as they were, many of them. They asked him, "How shall we pray?" He gave them the Lord's Prayer. He, God-man that he was, told them no other prayer. . . . Entire books have been written about the Lord's Prayer but there is no mention of books in Brother Lawrence's reported conversations and letters. His serenity, his simplicity is that of the Prayer.

Brother Lawrence's times were no different from ours. St. Teresa of Avila, who lived in the time of the Inquisition, wrote, "All times are dangerous times." Just as St. Paul called upon us to be other Christs, Lawrence was another Christ, who lived in the presence of the Father at all times.

He grew up like other children and young men, and went through a conversion of heart at the age of sixteen. He had one of those striking experiences that I think we all have, whether we live in the country or in the city. "One winter day he noticed a tree stripped of its leaves and reflected that before long leaves would appear anew, then flowers and then the fruit, and that this consideration gave him so striking an idea of the Providence and might of God that it had never since been effaced from his soul; . . . and kindled in him so great a love for God that he was not able to say if it had at all increased during the forty-odd years which had since passed."

We have to leap into faith through the senses—from the natural to the supernatural—and I was drawn to the Church in my youth because it appealed to the senses. The music speaking to the ear, the incense to the sense of smell, the appeal of color to the eye, stained glass, ikons and statues, the bread and wine to the taste, the touch of rich vestments and altar linens, the touch of holy water, oils, the sign of the cross, the beating of the breast.

When my own mother was dying, she asked me quietly and soberly, "What about a future life?" I could only point to the flowers which surrounded her. It was in the fall and there were giant chrysanthemums filling the tables in her room. It was like a promise from God, and God keeps his promises. I pointed to the trees outside, stripped of their leaves, looking dead to the eye from that distance, but there had recently been a blaze of glory in the color of the maples. Another sign of a promise. Later she said, "I can only pray the Our Father and the Creed. Is that enough?" And when I thought of the books, which would fill libraries, that had been written on every phrase contained in the Our Father, it comforted my heart to know that she was practicing the presence of God this way.

The Practice of the Presence of God consists of conversations, letters, and maxims on how we should live, with the idea of cultivating this sense of the presence of God in the soul, and indeed in the world about us.

The very word "sense" might seem to throw us off, because the whole book has to do with the spiritual life of man, not his sense life, and so can be brushed aside as nonsense. But we all have a desire for the True, the Good, and the Beautiful which is God. And we look around us today in a time of war and fear, of stockpiling for war, of greed, dishonesty, and ambition, and long for peace in our time, for that peace which passeth understanding, which we see only in glimpses, through a glass darkly.

When St. Paul says to pray always, to pray without ceasing, he is also talking about practicing the presence of God.

A few years ago an old woman died in our midst, here at our House of Hospitality in New York. She was surrounded by many men and women she had known a long time; she had the best of care. We had a nurse living with us who could meet any emergency. But Catherine, in the last few weeks of her life, often clutched at my hand as I passed her, and would plead with me: "There is a God, tell me there is a God! Tell me!"

I could only say, "Yes, Catherine, there is a God. He is our Father and He loves us, you and me." When you say these things it is an act of faith. You feel your helplessness so you pray harder. You seem to know nothing, you can only hold her hand and make your affirmation. So much of our prayer is made up of these affirmations. "I praise Thee, O

God, I bless Thee. What have I on earth but Thee and what do I desire in heaven besides Thee?" I am saying this *for* Catherine, *instead* of Catherine, because she is in "the valley of the shadow."

But did I comfort her? A few days later a young girl said to me, "The word *Father* means nothing to me. It brings me no comfort. I had a drunken father who abused my mother and beat his children." We can do nothing by our words. So we are driven to prayer by our helplessness. God takes over.

Living today in a time of war, crying out Peace, Peace when there is no Peace, fearing age and death, pain and darkness, destitution and loneliness, people need to get back to the simplicity of Brother Lawrence. . . .

We need this book today when we are overwhelmed by the vastness of today's problems. We need to return to the simplicity of a Brother Lawrence, whose "little way" makes our burdens light and rejoices the heart.

These days I can never look up at the sky and see the moon without thinking with wonder and awe that men have walked there. To conceive of such a thing—to desire such an adventure, to be capable of overcoming all fear, all doubt, to have faith in man's ability to solve problems, and seek out the way to go about this great exploration—what dedication of mind and will! "What is man that thou are mindful of him? Thou hast made him little less than the angels." It keeps coming into my mind—how much man would be capable of if his soul were strong in the love of God, if he wanted God as much as he wanted to penetrate the power and glory of God's creation.

To know Him, to love Him, and to serve Him—a personal God, who took on human flesh and became man and suffered and died for us. To find the way, not to the moon but to God—this is man's real desire, because of his need for love, and God is love.

Brother Lawrence, who worked the last thirty years of his life in the kitchen of a Carmelite monastery and died at the age of 80 found Him in "The Practice of the Presence of God."

March–April 1976

I must recall the words again of St. Teresa—that the only way we can show our love for God is by our love for our fellows. And not an abstract love either. If I cannot remember and contemplate my own worse sins, hidden, and more subtle, then God help me! And if I cannot be patient under trials which the Lord compliments me by sending me, then all my other work is vain. It is not by editing a paper or by writing and speaking that I am going to do penance and achieve sanctity. But by being truly loving and gentle and peaceful in the midst of trouble. [Fr. Louis] Lallemant says that when we are comfortable, beware. It is only when things are hard that we are making progress. God is good to send trials. They are a special mark of love.

[Jean-Pierre de] Caussade says that those circumstances which surround us are the very ones God wills for us.

Dear Lord, keep us from pride and self-will! Help us to love one another. It is easy to love saints. What do we know about each other's inward struggles?

"Love in action is a harsh and dreadful thing compared with love in dreams."—Fr. Zosima in *The Brothers Karamazov*.
House of Hospitality

What do I talk to myself about? When I am truly alone, with no babies around, as when I am in church alone, I pray. I say the rosary, I read my psalms, make the Acts: adoration, contrition, thanksgiving, supplication. And there is time. At home, kneeling by my bed, or in the bitter cold saying my prayers in bed, they are brief, half conscious, and the planning, the considering, the figuring of ways of "making ends meet" goes on. Until I catch myself and turn to God again.

"All these things shall be added unto you." "He knoweth that ye have need of these things." St. Teresa of Avila says we should not trouble our Lord with such petty trifles. We should ask great things of Him.

So I pray for Russia, for our own country, for our fellowmen, our fellow workers, for the sick, the starving, the dying, the dead.

January 1948, *On Pilgrimage*

Meditations for women, these notes should be called, jumping as I do from the profane to the sacred over and over. But then, living in the country, with little children, with growing things, one has the sacramental view of life. All things are His and all are holy.

I used to wish I could get away from my habit of constant, undisciplined reading, but in the family one certainly is cured of it. If you stop to read a paper, pick up a book, the children are into the tubs or the sewing machine drawers. And as for praying with a book—there has been none of that this Lent for me. Everything is interrupted, even prayers, since by nightfall one is too tired to pray with understanding. So I try to practice the presence of God after the manner of Blessed Lawrence, and pray without ceasing, as St. Paul advised. He might even have had women in mind. But he himself was active enough, weaving goat hair into tents and sail cloth to earn a living, and preaching nights and Sundays. So I am trying to learn to recall my soul like the straying creature it is as it wanders off over and over again during the day, and lift my heart to the Blessed Mother and

His saints, since my occupations are the lowly and humble ones as were theirs.

March 1948, *On Pilgrimage*

Despite my feelings of almost hopelessness and desperation, humanly speaking, I came through the day feeling singularly calm, peaceful, and happy.

Three conclusions were the result of my praying. First: My getting into a temper helped nobody. But remaining loving toward all helped to calm them all. Hence a great responsibility rests on me. Second: it was cruel to be harsh to anyone so absolutely dependent as they are, humanly, on my kindness. Third: it is a healthy sign that they are not crushed and humble toward other human beings by their own miseries. I mean, going around meekly for fear of me, or being humble out of human respect.

One must be humble only from a divine motive, otherwise humility is a debasing and repulsive attitude. To be humble and meek because your bread and butter depends on it is awful. It is to lose one's sense of human dignity.

Let reform come through love of God only and from that love of God, love of each other. . . .

The aftereffects of last night's and this morning's heavy praying have been peace and joy and strength and thanksgiving and a great deal of humility, too, at being so weak that God had to send me consolation to prepare me for the next trial.

House of Hospitality

One of the peculiar enjoyments I got out of jail was in being on the other side for a change. Working in a laundry, for instance, ironing, mending the uniforms of jailers. For so many years I had been in charge of work, had been the administrator! It is too easy to forget that all we give is given to us to give. Nothing is ours. All we have to give is our time and patience, our love. How often we have failed in love, how often we have been brusque, cold, and indifferent. . . .

But in jail it was I who was getting pushed about. I was told what I could or could not do, hemmed in by rules and regulations and red tape and bureaucracy. It made me see my faults, but it also made me see how much more we accomplish at the Catholic Worker by not asking questions or doing any investigating but by cultivating a spirit of trust. The whole jail experience was good for my soul. I realized again how much ordinary kindness can do.

Loaves and Fishes

There is of course much fear in the world today and a sense of imminent disaster threatening. When St. Ignatius was asked what he would do if he were told he would die in an hour, he said that he would go right on doing what he was doing.

So we too, if we have a sense of Divine Providence, and abandon ourselves to it, will go on doing what we are doing, "the duties of our state in life," of our vocation.

The world is very beautiful around us these days and there are glimpses of heaven here and now. Of course we love this life and the joys of music and sunlight and children's laughter. But we know too that "the ear is not satisfied with hearing, nor the eye with seeing." But we know also that "eye hath not seen nor ear heard what God hath prepared for those who love Him." All things happen only by His permissive will and "all things work together for good to those who love God." So we pray for that—that we learn to love, that we grow in love.

October 1961

REVELATIONS

Dorothy often experienced moments of insight, clarity, or consolation, when life was clothed in a heightened sense of reality, and "the path seemed straighter." She recorded such experiences and tried to remember them when she was inclined to forget.

We have all probably noted those sudden moments of quiet—those strange and almost miraculous moments in the life of a big city when there is a cessation of traffic noises—just an instant when there is only the sound of footsteps which serves to emphasize a sudden peace. During those seconds it is possible to notice the sunlight, to notice our fellow humans, to take breath.

After hours of excitement and action and many human contacts, when even in one's sleep and at moments of waking there is a sense of the imminence of things to be done and of conflict ahead, it is good to seek those moments of perfect stillness and refreshment during early Mass.

Then indeed it seems that God touches the heart and the mind. There are moments of recollection, of realization when the path seems straighter, the course to be followed perfectly plain, though not easy. It is as though the great Physician to whom we go for healing had put straight that which was dislocated, and prescribed a course of action so definite that we breathe relief at having matters taken out of our hands.

Such a moment came this morning with the thought—the revolution we are engaged in is a lonely revolution, fought out in our own hearts, a struggle between Nature and Grace. It is the most important work of all in which we are engaged.

If we concentrate our energies primarily on that, then

we can trust those impulses of the Holy Spirit and follow them simply, without question. We can trust and believe that all things will work together for good to them that love God, and that He will guide and direct us in our work. We will accomplish just what he wishes us to accomplish and no more, regardless of our striving. Since we have good will, one need no longer worry as though the work depended just on ourselves.

"Christmas," December 1934

As I waited for the traffic light to change on my way to the Seamen's Defense Committee headquarters, I was idly saying my rosary, which was handy in my pocket. The recitation was more or less automatic, when suddenly like a bright light, like a joyful thought, the words Our Father pierced my heart. To all those who were about me, to all the passersby, to the longshoremen idling about the corner, black and white, to the striking seamen I was going to see, I was a kin, for we were all children of a common Father, all creatures of One Creator, and Catholic or Protestant, Jew or Christian, Communist or non-Communist, were bound together by this tie. We cannot escape the recognition of the fact that we are all brothers. Whether or not a man believes in Jesus Christ, His Incarnation, His Life here with us, His Crucifixion and Resurrection; whether or not a man believes in God, the fact remains that we are all children of one Father.

Meditation on this fact makes hatred and strife between brothers the more to be opposed. The work we must do is to strive for peace and concordance rather than hatred and strife.

November 1936

When the burdens pile high and the weight of all the responsibilities we have undertaken bows us down, when there are never enough beds to go around and never enough food on the table—then it is good to sit out in the cool of the evening with all our neighbors and exchange talk about babies and watch the adventurous life of the street.

The world is bowed down with grief, and in many ways God tries to bring us joy, and peace. They may seem at first to be little ways but if our hearts are right they color all our days and dispel the gray of the sadness of the times.

September 1939

It is good to think of the men in all the houses who cook, wash dishes, scrub, launder, ministering to others—all of them part of the Catholic Worker movement. To try to convey to them the glimpse of the "whole," this is a hard job. We all see only part. We all see through a glass darkly. Some see more clearly than others. Our joy in the work increases with our vision of the whole. Just as when a man, using his whole body in his work, is in better health than when he uses just head or hand alone. Workers must be scholars and scholars workers, as Peter says.

Heaven is when we see God face to face, when we shall see Him as He is. Now it is only a glimpse, a suggestion of light, of joy, of unity, of completion.

February 1940

One time I was traveling and far from home and lonely, and I awoke in the night almost on the verge of weeping with a sense of futility, of being unloved and unwanted. And suddenly the thought came to me of my importance as a daughter of God, daughter of a King, and I felt a sureness of God's love and at the same time a conviction that one of the greatest injustices, if one can put it that way, which one can do to God is to distrust His love, not realize His love. God so loved me that He gave His only begotten son. "If a mother will forget her children, never will I forget thee." Such tenderness. And with such complete ingratitude we forget the Father and His love!

July–August 1948, *On Pilgrimage*

Last night coming home on the ferry there was a heavy swell and a steady east wind. The taste of the salt spray was on my lips, and the sense of being upheld on the water reminded me of "the everlasting arms" which sustain us. Gulls wheeled overhead, grey and blue against the dark sea. On the Brooklyn shore the setting sun shone red in the windows of the warehouses and piers. It was after rush hour and there were not many on the boat. It was a half hour interlude of peace and silence and refreshment. May the many who come to us on the island feel this calm and strength and healing power of the sea, and may it lift them to God as it has so often lifted me.

September 1950

One afternoon on a walk I stood there and listened to the crows and starlings and the chatter of the little brook over iced stones and grasses and had my fill of beauty for an hour before I had to go back to the city again.

What a hunger, what a need we have for beauty and happiness that comes with beauty!

Irene pointed out a phrase to me recently of Ruskin's which appealed to us both. It was "the duty of delight." To reverence and be thankful for life itself, in a time when the world holds human life so lightly there is again joy. To be grateful is to be full of grace and grace is participation in the divine life, knowing that we are sons of God and heirs of the kingdom.

Happiness too means warmth after cold, peace after pain, and satisfaction after hunger. These simple joys are good to remember, too, especially for a woman, the home-maker. The works of mercy deal in such joys. I was reading a story of Dorothy Canfield in which a woman was speaking of her empty arms. A woman's arms need never be empty. Nor hands idle. There are always sick, the old, the little children to be cared for. And with love. We must express it with sweetness, with tenderness. When I saw the altar boy kiss the cruet of water this morning at Mass, I felt how necessary ritual is to life. To kiss the earth, to lift the arms, to embrace the lonely.

It seems to me I have written these things so many times before, for my own instruction and consolation, too. But it is a good time of year for thinking of these things, the beginning of Lent when we should rejoice to fast and pray and give alms.

February 1951

One night many years ago in a lonely moment, in a little town in Arkansas, I woke up with a terrible sense of futility and helplessness. I thought, "What am I doing traveling around speaking? Who am I anyway to be so presumptuous?" And suddenly a most wonderful sense of the glory of being a child of God swept over me, so joyous a sense of my own importance that I have often reflected on it since.

I would pray that our readers have it, and grow in it, this sense of their importance as temples of the Holy Ghost, sons of God, divinized by His coming. All things are possible to us, we can do all things in Him who strengthens us. We may look at the George Washington Bridge, great dams in the process of construction, airports, men flying, smashing atoms, deeply plunging into this material world to discover the secrets of the material universe and we may return refreshed to the Gospel which is the tiny mustard seed growing into a great tree throughout the world. . . .

January 1954

Ammon [Hennacy] had used some of the money from the sale of his book to take me to [Chekhov's] *The Three Sisters, The Cherry Orchard,* and last week to *Uncle Vanya.* In all of the plays there is a curious emphasis on work—the need of the human being to work in order to redeem himself and achieve some measure of happiness and satisfaction out of life. We are living in an age when there is such a sense of futility and purposelessness, such a sense of individual frustration, that these plays are curiously apt. That is why they have achieved such popularity. . . .

On the one hand to be humble, to acknowledge oneself a "grain of sand," as St. Thérèse used to say—"dust thou art and unto dust thou shalt return"—and on the other hand to recognize one's dignity as a son of God, with particular talents and vocations, which must be developed. To know that each one has his own contribution to make to our age, that none else can make, and work is necessary to develop it! How many writers, teachers, doctors, musicians, singers, there are among us who have not developed their capacities for lack of some spirit, some energy, some sense of the importance of what each one has to do! I know this very well, and I am sure other writers do, this need to prod oneself on to work. The closing lines of *Uncle Vanya* are most appealing. Sonya says,

> There is nothing for it. We must go on living! We shall go on living, Uncle Vanya. We shall live through a long, long chain of days and weary evenings; we shall patiently bear the trials that fate sends us; we shall

work for others, both now and in our old age and have no rest; and when our time comes we shall die without a murmur, and there beyond the grave we shall say that we have suffered, that we have wept, that life has been bitter to us, and God will have pity on us, and you and I, Uncle, dear Uncle, shall see a life that is bright, lovely, beautiful. We shall rejoice and look back at these troubles of ours with tenderness, with a smile—and we shall rest. I have faith, Uncle; I have fervent passionate faith. We shall rest.

And the old nurse goes on with her knitting, and the intellectual old mother goes on reading her pamphlet, and Sonya kneels by her uncle's side and comforts him in his unhappy love, and the deserted husband who has supported his wife, her lover, and their children, like Osee of old, sits to one side, playing on his guitar.

Neither Turgenev nor Chekhov, those great masters of short story and play, commit themselves, but they write of people of faith with such tenderness, such beauty, that one could almost say they believed, because they wished to believe.

March 1956

Christ said, I am the way, the Truth, the life. The trouble is, He is so hard to find. There is so little time, and the danger is so great that we will die before we have begun to live, spiritually speaking of course. (Because as I write that sentence, I can think of three people who have lamented to me that they have never lived, have had no experience, have never been fulfilled, are unwanted, rejected, and so on, with infinite sadness.) They are not talking about the spiritual life, but the life of the senses. They do not realize how universal is their complaint, "lest having Him they may have naught beside." And they flee the Hound of Heaven, because they do not want Him just yet. They are like St. Augustine, saying, "Give me purity, O Lord, but not yet." Because they cannot give up their love or their desire for love, and that intensity of life, which comes with love. They do not believe Him when He says, "I have come to bring life, and to bring it more abundantly."

There are times in our lives when we feel life flow in our veins, feel ourselves to be alive, we can look into our hearts and find there the Holy Trinity, the indwelling of the Holy Spirit. But we need to be alone, we need to have time, to be at rest, to be rested too.

We need to sleep, we need to rest, we need to lose consciousness, to die in this way, in order to live—and this is on the natural plane. But grace builds on nature, and we must live a good natural life in order to lead the supernatural life to its fullest.

Baron von Hügel used to say that every morning as he made his plans for the day, he used to draw up a schedule of work to be done, and then cut half of it out. I should do the same about reading—draw up a list of books to be read, and then cut half of them out.

There is a time to do nothing, when one needs to do nothing, and now for me is one of those times.

July 1956

"Wisdom is the most active of all active things." This comes from the book of Wisdom, an apocryphal book in the Protestant Old Testament.

I had some glimpse of this when I had what I like to call a revelation, the second in my life. The first one, I tell it to show how materialistic, how selfish, how rooted in pride my inspirations, my revelations are, was when a sudden burst of happiness came over me at the discovery that I could earn my own living! I was seventeen and a freshman at the University of Illinois, working for board and room. I had to give 4 hours a day for that board and room, and I got 20 cents an hour for ironing clothes, or scrubbing a kitchen floor, or babysitting. I can still remember the exultation I felt. Exaltation, I might say. I had got hold of a profound truth. I had found a "philosophy of work," a phrase which Peter Maurin liked to use years later. . . .

My next great insight, or revelation, came ten years later, roughly speaking, as I read St. Augustine's *Confessions.* I was 27, and my insight came, suddenly, as I was reading beside the waters of Raritan Bay. "No matter how old I get," I thought, with intense joy, "I will always have the torrents of pleasure promised in the Psalms that come from reading, from study, from the association with great and noble minds."

No matter how old I get (and I am 75 in Nov. 1972, this year), no matter how feeble, short of breath, incapable of walking more than a few blocks, what with heart murmurs, heart failures, emphysema perhaps, arthritis in feet and knees, with all these symptoms of age and decrepitude, my heart can still leap for joy as I read and suddenly assent to some great truth enunciated by some great mind and heart.

July 21, 1972, *Duty of Delight*

SAVED BY BEAUTY

Much of Dorothy's life was spent in city slums. Though she never became inured to the sights and smells of poverty, she remained keenly alert to signs of beauty, even cultivating the capacity to see beauty in places that others might overlook.

Often, she returned to Dostoevsky's line, "The world will be saved by beauty." This didn't mean the world would be saved by fine art or pretty things. It would be saved by our capacity to see beneath the surface, to see reality in its ultimate depth, as God sees it.

Some days when it rains, and the cellar is flooded and drowned rats, soaking newspapers, and old mattresses contribute a peculiar odor of decay, and the walls drip and the bannisters are slimy and the lights have to burn all day even on the top floor to dispel the gloom and one of the women has had one of her spells (for several days and nights), cursing and wailing—then it is indeed hard to love one another.

On other days, like this afternoon, when the sun is shining and the women have been cleaning house and washing clothes, everything looks bright and cozy and you forget the verminous walls. All you can see then are the nice things, the fact that the little fig tree in the window is covered with tiny figs, the milk bottle vase of forsythia is abloom, that someone has washed the windows, that Joe Cuellar keeps the office neat and clean, and that the sleeping quarters have clean bedding and that there is an empty bed for a guest and that the women are sitting companionably around the teapot in the front building and sharing buns.

The children shout in the streets with joy that winter is over and gone, the playground is open at night and the street is bright with people and lights, the sap is rising, one lives again after the cold and rain, the death of winter.

Then we can say with the poet Maxwell Bodenheim, "I know not ugliness. It is a mood which has forsaken me."

May 1950

I have fallen in love many a time in the fall of the year. I mean those times when body and soul are revived, and in the keen clear air of autumn after a hot exhausting summer, I felt new strength to see, to "know" clearly, and to love, to look upon my neighbor and to love. Almost to be taken out of myself. I do not mean being in love with a particular person. I mean that quality of in-loveness that may brush like a sweet fragrance, a sound faintly heard, a sense of the beauty of one particular human being, or even one aspect of life. It may be an intuition of immortality, of the glory of God, of His Presence in the world. But it is almost impossible to put into words. The point is that it is general rather than particular, though it may come as a reminder, this flash of understanding, of recognition, with the reading of a particular book, or hearing some strain of music.

It is tied up in some way also with the sense of hope, and an understanding of hope. How can we live without it, as a supernatural virtue, "hoping against hope," during this dark period of violence and suffering throughout the world?

I am bold in trying to express the inexpressible, to write of happiness, even of joy that comes, regardless of age, color, or condition of servitude to us all.

Regardless of failures, regardless even of the sufferings of others. If we did not have this hope, this joy, this love, how could we help others? How could we have the strength to hold on to them, to hold them up when they are drowning in sorrow, suffocating in blackness, almost letting go of life, life which we know with a sure knowledge is precious, which is something to hold to, be grateful for, to reverence.

This is the point of war protests, of a strong faith in the doctrine of nonviolence, the evidence of its continuing efficacy throughout the world.

It is the spiritual weapon of the little ones, the weak, the powerless, the poor. In some obscure way, an inarticulate way, the young have grasped this.

From this day on I am going to ask for the Holy Spirit and wait. I will be growing, of this I am sure. Maybe it won't come until the moment I die.

But how wonderful if we could be "surprised by joy," to use the title of C.S. Lewis's book. I have heard of witnesses who said, "When he or she died, at that moment a look of surprise" came over their faces, "surprised joy which was wonderful to behold."

October 1969, *The Duty of Delight*

The world will be saved by beauty, Dostoevsky wrote, and Solzhenitsyn quoted it in his Nobel talk. I look back on my childhood and remember beauty. The smell of sweet clover in a vacant lot, a hopeful clump of grass growing up through the cracks of a city pavement. A feather dropped from some pigeon. A stalking cat. Ruskin wrote of "the duty of delight," and told us to lift up our heads and see the cloud formations in the sky. I have seen sunrises at the foot of a New York street, coming up over the East River. I have always found a strange beauty in the suffering faces which surround us in the city. Black, brown, and grey heads bent over those bowls of food, that so necessary food which is always there at St. Joseph's House on First St., prepared each morning by Ed Forand or some of the young volunteers. We all enter into the act of hospitality, one way or another. So many of those who come in to eat return to serve, to become part of the "family."

September 1974

"Faith is the substance of things hoped for, the evidence of things not seen. . . . If, in this life only, we have hope in Christ, we are of all men the most miserable. Eye hath not seen, nor ear heard . . . the things which God hath prepared for those who love Him." What samples of His love in

Creation all around us! Even in the city, the changing sky, the trees, frail though they may be, which prisoners grow on Riker's Island, to be planted around the city, bear witness. People—all humankind, in some way.

"In the beginning, God created heaven and earth." Looking out over the bay, the gulls, the "paths in the sea," the tiny ripples stirring a patch of water here and there, the reflections of clouds on the surface—how beautiful it all is.

I love postal cards. This week I was given one of birch trees from Aspen, Colorado—a beauty. Mary Roberts, at Cabrini Center, sent me one of St. Francis in ecstasy by Bellini. Her note was as beautiful as her card. She is a "lover of beautifulness" (a phrase I think is Scriptural).

Alone all day. A sudden storm in the night. Vast, dark clouds and a glaring, lightning flash with thunder. No rain. Reading *Dr. Zhivago* a second time.

July–August 1977

There is poverty and hunger and war in the world, and preparations for more war. There is desperate suffering, with no prospects of relief. Yet, countries are making armaments. They are using the money that should feed and care for the poor to make instruments of death for the young and healthy.

But we would be contributing to the misery and desperation of the world if we failed to rejoice in the sun, the moon, and the stars, in the rivers which surround this island on which we live, in the cool breezes on the bay, in what food we have, and in the benefactors God sends.

St. Teresa of Avila, whose feast falls in October, said she had so grateful a heart that she could be bought (I suppose she meant her gratitude could be bought) with a sardine. Another time, she said, they were so poor they didn't have sticks to make a fire to cook a sardine—if they had a sardine.

But she also said, fiercely, that she would rather the walls of her convents fall in on them than that they should lose Holy Poverty. So, we are not asking you to take away from us that great gift, we are just asking you to keep the work going.

So, we are begging you again for loaves and fishes, or the money to buy them. And, since we know the Lord will multiply them for us, as He always has in the past, we are thanking you now.

"Fall Appeal," October–November 1978

7

Love Is the Measure

"The man I loved, with whom I entered into a common-law marriage, was an anarchist, an Englishman by descent, and a biologist." So, in The Long Loneliness, *Dorothy introduced Forster Batterham, her "common-law husband," who became the father of her child. Though she writes that he considered their relationship a "comradeship," and "always rebelled against the institution of the family and the tyranny of love," there is no doubt of Dorothy's own feelings. "I loved him for all he knew and pitied him for all he didn't know. I loved him for the odds and ends I had to fish out of his sweater pockets and for the sand and shells he brought in with his fishing. I loved his lean cold body as he got into bed smelling of the sea and I loved his integrity and stubborn pride." And this very experience of "natural happiness," culminating in the birth of her daughter, caused her love to overflow. "Forster had made the physical world come alive for me, and had awakened in my heart a flood of gratitude. The final object of this love and gratitude was God."*

After her decision to have Tamar baptized, a step she followed a year later, she found it necessary to separate from Forster, whose "integrity and stubborn pride" excluded the possibility of marriage. As her letters over the next years make clear, she maintained the hope that this separation was not irrevocable. She continued to profess her love and tried by every means to persuade him to "get over his pig-headedness" and agree to marry. "The ache in my heart is intolerable at times, and sometimes for days I can feel

*your lips upon me, waking and sleeping. It is because I love you
so much that I want you to marry me." But it was not to be. She
acknowledged this in a final letter in December 1932, the same
month that she offered her prayer at the Shrine of the Immaculate
Conception "with tears and with anguish" to find her vocation; the
same month when she met Peter Maurin, who pointed her toward
founding the Catholic Worker, and whose ideas dominated the rest
of her life.*

*At the time of her conversion, Dorothy wrote, some of her radi-
cal friends insinuated that her turn to God was because she was
"tired of sex, satiated, disillusioned." But this was quite far from
her feelings. "It was because through a whole love, both physical
and spiritual, I came to know God."*

*Love in its various forms remained a central theme in Doro-
thy's writings. And as the reflections below indicate, she continued
to insist on the continuity between natural love in all its dimensions and the love of God. In all cases, such love entailed both joy
and suffering.*

*Above all, Dorothy believed, when we love another person it
means seeing Christ in them—their true, best self. And sometimes
this involved an act of the will. "If you will to love someone, you
soon do. You will to love this cranky old man, and someday you do.
It depends on how hard you try."*

*In the words of St. John of the Cross, which she liked to repeat,
"Where there is no love, put love, and you will draw love out."
And "Love is the measure by which we shall be judged."*

The great commandment which comprises all others is to
love one another. If we do this we fulfill the law. How can
we love God whom we have not seen, if we do not love our
fellows whom we do see? But of course it is hard to love our
fellowman. Father Zosima in *The Brothers Karamazov* said,
"Love in practice is a harsh and dreadful thing compared
to love in dreams." He was talking of a great humanitarian

who said the further away from people she was, the more she could love them. There are some people whom it is easy to love. God in his goodness has given the heart of man the capacity for human love and it is good to compare this love between a betrothed man and woman and the love we are to bear each other. Love makes all things easy.

When one loves, there is, at that time, a correlation between the spiritual and the material. Even the flesh itself is energized, the human spirit is made strong. All sacrifice, all suffering is easy for the sake of love. A mother will endure all-night vigils by the bedside of a sick child. With every child that is born to her, born in anguish that is quickly forgotten, and all too small a price to pay, her heart is enlarged to take another in. Strength and endurance and courage are granted to her with the love she bears those near and dear to her. When we hear of parents failing in this faithfulness we are repelled as by something "unnatural." If natural love can be so great, and we must remember that grace builds upon nature, then how great should be the supernatural love we should bear our fellows. It is this love which will solve all problems, family, national, international.

"Hell Is Not to Love Any More," May 1939

A Foretaste of Heaven

Whenever I groan within myself and think how hard it is to keep writing about love in these times of tension and strife, which may at any moment become for us all a time of terror, I think to myself, "What else is the world interested in?" What else do we all want, each one of us, except to love and be loved, in our families, in our work, in all our relationships? God is Love. Love casts out fear. Even the most ardent revolutionist, seeking to change the world, to overturn the tables of the money changers, is trying to make a world where it is easier for people to love, to stand in that relationship to each other. We want with all our hearts to love, to be loved. And not just in the family but to look upon all as our mothers, sisters, brothers, children. It is when we love the most intensely and most humanly that we can recognize how tepid is our love for others. The keenness and intensity of love brings with it suffering, of course, but joy too, because it is a foretaste of heaven. I often think in relation to my love for little Becky, Susie, and Eric [Tamar's children]: "That is the way I must love every child and want to serve them, cherish them, and protect them." Even that relationship which is set off from other loves by that slight change in phraseology (instead of "loving," one is "in love")—the very change in terminology, denoting a living in love, a dwelling in love at all times, being bathed in love, so that every waking thought, word, deed, and suffering is permeated by that love—yes, that relationship above all should give us not only a taste of the love of God for us but the kind of love we should have for all.

When you love people, you see all the good in them, all the Christ in them. God sees Christ, His Son, in us and loves us. And so we should see Christ in others, *and nothing else,* and love them. There can never be enough of it. There can never be enough thinking about it. St. John of the Cross said that where there was no love, put love and you would take out love. The principle certainly works. I've seen my friend, Sister Peter Claver, with that warm friendliness of hers which is partly natural but which is intensified and made enduring by grace, come into a place which is cold with tension and conflict, and warm the house with her love.

And this is not easy. Everyone will try to kill that love in you, even your nearest and dearest; at least they will try to prune it. "Don't you know this, that, and the other thing about this person? He or she did this. If you don't want to hear it, you must hear. It is for your good to hear it. It is my duty to tell you, and it is your duty to take recognition of it. You must stop loving, modify your loving, show your disapproval. You cannot possibly love—if you pretend you do, you are a hypocrite, and the truth is not in you. You are contributing to the delinquency of that person by your sentimental blindness. It is such people as you who add to the sum total of confusion and wickedness and soft appeasement and compromise and the policy of expediency in this world. You are to blame for communism, for industrial capitalism, and finally for hell on earth."

The antagonism often rises to a crescendo of vituperation, an intensification of opposition on all sides. You are quite borne down by it. And the only Christian answer is *love*, to the very end, to the laying down of your life.

To see only the good, the Christ, in others! . . . How many people are dying and going to God their Father and saying sadly, "We have not so much as heard that there is a Holy Spirit." And how will they hear if none preaches to them? And what kind of shepherds have many of them had? Ezekiel said in his day, "Woe to the shepherds that feed themselves and not their sheep!" . . .

It is an easy thing to talk about love, but it is something to be proven, to be suffered, to be learned. That's why we have our retreat house at Newburgh. . . .

It is always a terrible thing to come back to Mott Street. To come back in a driving rain, to men crouched on the stairs, huddled in doorways, without overcoats because they sold them perhaps the week before when it was warm, to satisfy hunger or thirst—who knows? Those without love would say, "It serves them right, drinking up their clothes." God help us if we got just what we deserved!

April 1948, *On Pilgrimage*

Willing to Love

This morning between conferences I wept, partly for joy and partly for the misery of life, partly at being so overwhelmed with demands made upon me, and partly with fatigue and nerves. [The number of people demanding attention, banging on my door at midnight.] And the burden gets too heavy; there are too many of them; my love is too small; I even feel with terror, "I have no love in my heart; I have nothing to give them." And yet I have to pretend I have.

But strange and wonderful, the make-believe becomes true. If you will to love someone, you soon do. You will to love this cranky old man, and someday you do. It depends on how hard you try.

How much there is to learn of love, that feeling of the body and soul, that teaches us what God is, that He is love.

"Notes from a Retreat,"
July–August 1948,
On Pilgrimage

• A New Commandment

There is a character in *The Plague*, by Albert Camus, who says that he is tired of hearing about men dying for an idea. He would like to hear about a man dying for love for a change. He goes on to say that men have forgotten how to love, that all they seem to be thinking of these days is learning how to kill. Man, he says, seems to have lost the capacity for love.

What is God but Love? What is a religion without love? We read of the saints dying for love, and we wonder what they mean. There was a silly verse I used to hear long ago: "Men have died from time to time, and worms have eaten them, but not for love." It comes from *As You Like It*. And nowadays in this time of war and preparing for war, we would agree, except for the saints. Yes, they have died for love of God. But Camus's character would say, "I mean for love of man." Our Lord did that, but most people no longer believe in Him. It is hard to talk to people about God if they do not believe in Him. So one can talk and write of love. People want to believe in that even when they are all but convinced that it is an illusion. (It would be better still to love rather than to write about it. It would be more convincing.)

In the Old and New Testaments there are various ways in which the relationship of God and men [is] mentioned. There is the shepherd and his sheep. "The Lord is my shepherd." "I am the Good Shepherd." The animal and the man. There is the servant and the master, there is the son and the father, and there is the bride and the bridegroom. "Behold, the bridegroom cometh." The Song of Songs, the Canticle of Canticles, is all about love. "Let Him kiss me with the kisses of His mouth."

It is hard to believe in this love. In a book by Hugh of St. Victor, which I read once on the way from St. Paul to Chicago, there is a conversation between the soul and God about this love. The soul is petulant and wants to know what kind of a love is that which loves everyone indiscriminately, the thief and the Samaritan, the wife and the mother and the harlot? The soul complains that it wishes a *particular* love, a love for herself alone. And God replies fondly that, after all, since no two people are alike in this world, He has indeed a particular fondness for each one of us, an exclusive love to satisfy each one alone.

It is hard to believe in this love because it is a tremendous love. "It is a terrible thing to fall into the hands of the living God." If we do once catch a glimpse of it, we are afraid of it. Once we recognize that we are sons of God, that the seed of divine life has been planted in us at baptism, we are overcome by that obligation placed upon us of growing in the love of God. And what we do not do voluntarily, He will do for us. . . .

If we cannot deny the *self* in us, kill the self-love, as He has commanded, and put on the Christ life, then God will do it for us. We must become like Him. Love must go through these purgations.

Unfortunately, when we speak of the human love of man and woman, most people, though they hope against hope, still regard it as an illusion, a great and glowing experience, a magic which comes into their lives for the sake of the pro-creation of the race. They assume and accept the fact that it will die, that it will not last, and in their vain clutching at it, they will put off one partner and look for it in another, and so the sad game goes on, with our movie stars going from the fifth to the sixth bride and swearing the selfsame promises to each.

That most people in America look upon love as an illusion would seem to be evidenced by the many divorces we see today—and the sensuality of despair that exists all around us. But all these divorces may too be an evidence about love. They hear very little of it in this war-torn world, and they are all seeking it. Pascal said of love, "You would not seek me if you had not already found me." Just so much faith is there, at any rate. A faith in love, a seeking for love. It is something, then, to build on, amongst the mass of people who have lost God, who do not know in what they believe, though they believe in and seek for love.

And where are the teachers to teach of this love, of the stages of this love, the purgations of this love, the sufferings entailed by this love, the stages through which natural love must pass to reach the supernatural?

We would all like to hear of men laying down their lives for love for their fellows, and we do not want to hear of it in the heroic tones of a statesman or a prince of the church. We all know that such phrases used in wartime mean nothing. Men are taught to kill, not to lay down their lives if they can possibly help it. Of course we do not talk of brothers in wartime. We talk of the enemy, and we forget the Beatitudes and the commandment to love our enemy, do good to them that persecute us. "A new commandment I give you, that you love one another as I have loved you." One said that who did lay down His life for all men.

Youth demands the heroic, Claudel said, and youth likes to dream of heroic deeds and of firing squads, of martyrs and of high adventure. But bread means life too; and money, which buys bread, for which we work, also means life. Sharing and community living mean laying down your life for your fellows also. True love is delicate and kind, full of gentle perception and understanding, full of beauty and grace, full of joy unutterable. Eye hath not seen, nor ear heard, what God hath prepared for those who love Him.

And there should be some flavor of this in all our love for others. We are all one. We are *one flesh* in the Mystical Body, as man and woman are said to be one flesh in marriage. With such a love one would see all things new; we would begin to see people as they really are, as God sees them.

We may be living in a desert when it comes to such perceptions now, and that desert may stretch out before us for years. But a thousand years are as one day in the sight of God, and soon we will know as we are known. Until then, we will have glimpses of brotherhood in play, in suffering, in serving, and we will begin to train for that community, that communion, that Father Henri Perrin, SJ, talked so much about in his story of the worker priest in Germany.

November 1948, *On Pilgrimage*

To See Christ in Others

On the one hand, there is the sadness of the world—and on the other hand, when I went to church today and the place was flooded with sunshine, and it was a clear, cold day outside . . . suddenly my heart was so flooded with joy and thankfulness and so overwhelmed at the beauty and the glory and the majesty of our God. . . .

The immanence of God in all things! "In Him we live and move and have our being" (Acts 17:28). "He is not far from every one of us" (Acts 17:27).

To love with understanding and without understanding. To love blindly, and to folly. To see only what is lovable. To think only on these things. To see the best in everyone around, their virtues rather than their faults. To see Christ in them.

December 1948, *On Pilgrimage*

A Love That Looks like Folly

Our pacifism must be a complete pacifism, and our love must grow in strength to overcome bitterness and resentments. Yesterday while I prayed in our parish church, there was a baptism going on, and I thought how close the priests were to our hearts—how they came to us in all the most holy and happy moments of our lives, birth and death and marriage, with the life-giving sacraments which their anointed hands alone could bring. And I thought too of the kind of love we should have for each other, if we were to see Christ in each other, a love which discounted the irascible remark, a confident love, a love which at times might look like folly indeed.

What more foolish a love is there than that portrayed in the gospel—the father for the prodigal son, the love of the shepherd for his sheep, the love which asked the servants to sit down so that the master could minister to them, wait upon them, wash their feet in a gesture of total and utter abandonment of love! And how far we are from it all!

Such a struggle going on shows how far we are from it, and how near to the surface class war is here in this country. There need be no Communist influence to fan the flame of resentment, the sense of injury which working men have been feeling over the years.

And in this struggle as in all the other varieties of war we have known, our job is to build up techniques of nonviolent resistance, using the force of love to overcome hatred, praying and suffering with our brothers in their conflicts.

April 1949

Happiness and Suffering

Another accusation is lodged at us—and that is that we see the misery of our life too clearly. We are always looking out of back doors. We see the rats that swarm the tenements, the vermin that crawl on the walls, the stench in the hallways of the poor, the garbage-filled gutters, the greasy moisture oozing from the walls of the cold tenements, the dirt and degradation of the human beings who throng every day, rain or shine, in long lines outside our door for soup and bread.

Any statement on our part that we love this life, that we would not be happy elsewhere, that we rejoice in such wretchedness, would lay us open to the charge of perverseness, of masochism, or most damning of all, of sentimentality.

And yet we do dare to say that this rejoicing is a measure of our love. To love is to be happy, and yet to love is also to suffer. To love the poor, one must be one with them. There is always the yearning for union, for the close embrace, even if it leads to depths unutterable. We must show our love for Christ by our love for the poor, so how can there help but be a rejoicing at the chance to show this love.

April 1950

Teaching Us to Love

It grows ever harder to talk of love in the face of a scorning world. We have not begun to learn the meaning of love, the strength of it, the joy of it. And I am afraid we are not going to learn it from reading the daily papers or considering the struggles that are taking place on the other side of the world and in the United Nations halls here at home.

We are the little ones, and we can only pray to the saints of our days, the little saints, to disclose to us this hidden world of the Gospel, this Hidden God, this pearl of great price, this kingdom of heaven within us. It is only then can we learn about love and rejoicing, and it is the meaning of life and its reward.

We talk of one world, and our common humanity, and the brotherhood of man, of principles of justice and freedom which befit the dignity of man, but from whence does he derive this dignity but that he is the son of God?

The one lesson which is reiterated over and over again is that we are one, we pray to be one, we want to love and suffer for each other, so let us pray and do penance in each little way that is offered us through the days, and God will then give us a heart of flesh to take away our heart of stone and with our prayers we can save all those dying each day, knowing that God will wipe away all tears from their eyes.

Lest these words which I write on my knees be scorned, know they are St. John's words, the apostle of love, who lived to see "charity grow cold" and who never ceased to cry out "my children, love one another."

It is the only word for Christmas when love came down to the mire, to teach us that love.

December 1950

8

Spiritual Counsel

"The reason we write," Dorothy noted, "is to communicate ideas. . . . We must overflow in writing about all the things we have been talking about and living during the month. Writing is an act of community. It is a letter, it is comforting, consoling, helping, advising on our part, as well as asking it on yours. It is a part of our human association with each other. It is an expression of our love and concern for each other."

If she regarded her columns in the paper as a kind of letter, it is fair to say that actual letter-writing was one of Dorothy's principal occupations. From her diary, we learn that she often spent several hours a day answering mail. Many of these letters were acknowledgments and thanks to benefactors, while others were simply a way of staying in touch with friends and fellow workers.

But often in her letters (published in All the Way to Heaven) she responded to the sorrows, doubts, and private struggles of her correspondents. To them Dorothy wrote with special care, offering compassion, exhortations to renewed faith, encouragement in their efforts to follow Christ. Sometimes she felt compelled to deliver a message her correspondents were not seeking. But in every case, she tried to impart a message of love. And in her private journals, she often applied the same compassion and frankness in counseling herself.

TO FRIENDS

To Catherine de Hueck

Catherine de Hueck (d. 1985) was a colorful and charismatic fig-ure whose career in some ways paralleled and at times overlapped with Dorothy's. A Russian baroness who fled the Soviet Union, she underwent a powerful conversion and afterward founded Friendship House in Toronto and also later in Harlem. She and Dorothy became lifelong friends. In this letter, Dorothy responded to Catherine's question: "How do you awaken Catholics? How do you bring them to the realization of their eternal destiny?"

After my month's absence in Washington and Pittsburgh, I return to find your letter, and I was glad to hear from you even though your letter sounded sad. . . . You sounded, too, so discouraged and you know as well as I do that discour-agement is a temptation of the devil. Why should we try to see results? It is enough to keep on in the face of what looks to be defeat. We certainly have enough examples in the lives of the saints to help us. Not to speak of that greatest of fail-ures (to the eyes of the world) of Christ on the cross. Why look for response? After all, we can only do what lies in our power and leave all the rest to God, and He will attend to it. You do not know yourself what you are doing, how far-reaching your influence is. I have heard people speak of you in different parts of the country. Why should you expect to see results in the shape of Houses of Friendship? Perhaps you are arousing in them instead the sense of personal responsibility. After all, God often lets us start doing one thing and many of the results we accomplish are incalcu-lably far-reaching, splendid in their own way, but quite dif-ferent from what we expected. Let us think only in terms of our own selves and God and not worry about anyone else.

Just had a long blast from Father Sullivan in which he

bawls hell out of me and tells me that those who are holding up the procession (meaning me and Peter) ought to get off the road—that he had wanted to follow a St. Joan, but that she would not get in the saddle, etc.

These are some of the things that are hard to bear. I do know exactly what I am doing. I know that Peter is a leader worthy to be followed. And no such blast is going to deter me from the program which we have mapped out for ourselves. Even if there is lack of unity amongst us, I just go straight ahead, doing the best I can with the very poor human material God sends. Just look at the kind of disciples He chose for Himself, and how little they understood Him, how they wanted a temporal kingdom and thought all was lost until the Descent of the Holy Ghost enlightened them. Why should we expect to be anything else but unprofitable servants? We simply have to leave things in God's hands. Get hold of *Abandonment to Divine Providence* by [Jean-Pierre de] Caussade and comfort yourself with that. It's done more to help me these past years than any other spiritual writer. In fact I could get along on the New Testament, the *Imitation [of Christ]* and Caussade for a long time and I am a pig about books. Spiritual reading is the oil that keeps the lamp burning, as you know.

August 9, 1936

Dorothy responded to the shocking news from Catherine that Friendship House was being closed by order of the Archbishop of Toronto. Among the reasons: the suggestion that Catherine was "a Communist boring from within," that she had absconded with funds, that she was an immoral, unworthy character, etc.

I should think you would feel privileged and happy to be sharing in some of our Lord's sufferings and above all not surprised as though it were something entirely unexpected.

What in the world do you expect? The very fact that there is all this obstruction and hindrance and trouble shows the work must be succeeding beyond your wildest hopes, otherwise the devil would not be putting so many hindrances in the way and trying to break down your morale. For that is surely what is being done. When you write in such terms as "I have fallen a hundred times to our Lord's three," I wonder at you. I wish to goodness I were up there to talk to you. You will think I am cold and unsympathetic, but really darling, I am not at all. I have been thinking of you constantly for the past week. I would hold your head up through it all and if you are deprived of any work to do, abandon yourself completely to divine providence, try to keep to ordinary routine as much as possible, and leave things in God's hands to work out.

If you are deprived completely of a means of earning a living and have no money for rent or food, I would quite simply throw myself on their charity, in your humility be a charge to them, instead of a person who has been taking a charge off the shoulders of others. But I would not flee from the scene of strife and persecution. I'd stay right there and face them out. Besides you are making a decision right in the heat of things which is never good. . . .

I purposely make this letter frank and sane as possible, because you are in such a state of mind. But at the same time, if you do not believe you have our love and sympathy, you are lacking in faith in us. We most truly believe, though, that the devil makes all this hullabaloo just when work is accomplishing the most good, so for that you should be most happy.

December 1936

To Stanley Vishnewski

Stanley, who joined the Catholic Worker as "a seventeen-year-old Lithuanian boy from the Williamsburg section of Brooklyn," was

one of the earliest and most faithful members of the CW family,
remaining until his death in 1979.

Got your letter this morning and hasten to write encouragement. I must get you Caussade's *Abandonment to Divine*
Providence to read which will convince you that God has
need of you being right where you are. Dryness and lack
of recollection can be good signs too, you know. God usually gives comfort to weak souls who need encouragement
and when they have progressed somewhat and He thinks
they are strong enough to bear it, He permits this dryness. If
you are faithful to your morning and evening prayers, and
make your morning offering, and carry your rosary in your
pocket so that you will remember to say even a part of it
every day, you will be getting along fine. If you have to force
yourself to pray, those prayers are of far more account with
God than any prayers which bring comfort with them. That
act of will is *very* important.

I cannot tell you how much we depend on you, Stanley,
so be cheered. You are very important to us. The very times
when you think that no progress is being made are usually
the best.

November 21, 1940

To a Catholic Worker

I have come to the conclusion that I have had so much natural love in my life for people that God is now proving me.
He is pruning down my natural love so that I may have
more supernatural love. And the love which comes out of
this daily dying is real and true and enduring. When I really
learn to love, then all these contradictions will cease. I do
truly realize that other people see all my faults more clearly
and they are quite rightly irritated by me.

Living around the CW is more like living in a refugee

camp than ever. In town we remain dirty, but the work goes on. . . .

December 6, 1944

To Jack English

Jack English, a former Catholic Worker, became a Trappist monk in Conyers, Georgia. Dorothy took great pride in him as the first religious vocation nourished by the movement, and she embraced him with deep maternal affection. Yet his struggles as an alcoholic caused him ongoing suffering. Dorothy counseled him from afar.

Tom [Sullivan] gave me your letter to read, since I knew about the affair, and for the life of me, I do not understand why you are in such a state now about it. As far as an experience goes, I know that every commandment in the book is broken, when it comes to drink. It all goes together. What really counts is your tremendous striving towards perfection. God has his hand on you, without doubt, and will not let you go. How else could anyone stay as long as you have in a Trappist monastery without special graces? The fearful thing will be if you do not correspond to them. That is the most terrifying line in St. Paul. That warning, that if we do not correspond to the graces we receive, they will be withdrawn from us.

The great wonder is that when we turn from God, He still holds to us so that we do not fall even lower. He has taken care of you with such infinite love, "prevented you with blessings of sweetness," to use the quaint old phrase in the *Imitation*.

Do hold on, from day to day, we need you there so. You are holding us up in ways you do not know. You with your flounderings are preventing others from falling.

What strength there is in going on just from hour to hour, day to day. You don't know anything about it, what is generated by that suffering. Of course you have to suffer to attain love. You may be just within grasp of Something and turn back.

It's like marriage, this going to orders. So many turn back, so many keep starting in again. Marriage, failure, divorce, remarriage and so on. What do we ever learn of love?

You have suffered so much, and each one's suffering is different. You have been brave in the past, to endure, and I am praying that you will be brave now and endure. I will be praying for you, and I will try to do some penance for you, I do not know exactly what, but I know that penance is needed as well as prayer. I will pray I have the grace to do penance—I am not very good at it. You know you have our love always. You are part of us around here.

August 21, 1952

I have such utter faith in you, Jack, that you are bearing a tremendous burden of temptation for us all, that you are sacrificing for us all. It is as though you are lightening our load so that we can endure here in the world. You surely have a vocation, I know it, and you never could have remained this long, you never could love it as you do.

Yesterday I had to drive the station wagon down for bread and it smelled of vomit and human excrement from the people sleeping in it at night. We spent the day scrubbing out the thing at the farm. Drunkenness and madness and filth and ugliness. A picture of hell. Just contrast that with your life down there.

And it is your prayers, your suffering, your temptations that enable us to bear things cheerfully, to spend hours in the chapel or in church, to keep up physically and mentally, to be happy, even.

Helene Iswolsky said she had some shattering spiritual experiences. Our life is shattering in a physical way, but gleams of spiritual joy come through it all. As I prayed for Fr. Kiely the other day, at 6 a.m. while he was talking drunkenly in the kitchen, I had a tremendous sense that Jesus, in his humanity, was present with us, that greater forces were being brought to play, that compared to this sum total of human weakness, struggled against (and they are all struggling, suffering) there were gigantic forces for good, great currents of grace set loose in the world like a mighty wind to purify and freshen the sin-laden atmosphere. It was like the breath of the sea, these thoughts, I was sure. I was sure we were doing what God wanted. And I am sure too, that you are holding us up, so be valiant.

December 31, 1953

Yours is a great suffering—I can see that, and of course we do not pick the particular kind of suffering we want to bear. But thank God you have some little burden of suffering to bear at this time when there is so much of it in the world. You are accounted worthy to suffer. When it dawns on us that this is a little coin the dear God is enriching us with to purchase salvation—our own and others—it ceases to be suffering. Remember, "Our infirmities were multiplied—afterward we made haste."

I've found that so many times. I was thinking, too, how often and how many of us feel unloved, unwanted, on many and many occasions during our lives—all the misunderstandings there are in families, even between husband and wife. We all want heaven here and now, no patience, no waiting. Don't think I don't understand how you feel, because I have felt the same many a time. How many times I have felt even a wall of hatred and resentment around me—sometimes over little things, and also over the big ones.

The opposition to the work, the idea that I did not understand or interpret Peter correctly. There really is not a soul around the CW who has not been the occasion of suffering. There has been many an occasion when I never wanted to see a CW again.

And then some such thought as that of St. John of the Cross would come, "Where there is no love, put love, and you will find love," and makes all right. When it comes down to it, even on the natural plane, it is much happier and more enlivening to love than to be loved.

November 28, 1956

To a Catholic Worker Friend
Who Suffered Many Sorrows

If we could only learn that the important thing is love, and that we will be judged on love—to keep on loving, and showing that love, and expressing that love, over and over, whether we feel it or not, seventy times seven, to mothers-in-law, to husbands, to children—and to be oblivious of insult, or hurt, or injury—not to see them, not to hear them. It is a hard, hard doctrine. I guess we get what we need in the way of discipline. God can change things in a twinkling of an eye. We have got to pray, to read the Gospel, to get to frequent communion, and not judge, not do anything, but love, love, love. A bitter lesson.

February 11, 1958

To a Friend in the Midwest

The terrible suffering we all have to go through, to prune and purify our love. I remember Fr. Farina says we must pass through the sorrowful mysteries to get to the glorious and most of us won't, we keep going back, trying to find the joyful again. We want to live in the honeymoon state always.

Anyway we do not know the heinousness of sin. We do not value grace, the most precious thing in the world. We are willful, so strongly willful, that God has to send all these things to us to cut us down, to prune us. We can only thank God He is doing it. And if it is the innocent who are suffering too (although who is without sin?), then we are suffering for the rest of the world, helping to bear the sum total of suffering, helping to expiate. Anyway we should be more thankful for suffering than we are.

I am writing this way, not so much for you, as for myself, to comfort myself too.

June 25, 1958

To a Catholic Worker Editor
Arrested for Aiding a Deserter

"Thou lovest justice and hateth iniquity, wherefore God, thy God, has anointed thee with the oil of gladness above thy companions."

May this be true of you this day.

Standing before a judge, appearing in court, is harder than a jail sentence. Whatever happens, I know God has you close to him. As for me, I know you were right to do exactly as you did, and do not worry about the overtones and exactitude of expression of what has already taken place. God takes care of everything, and rights our mistakes, makes straight our paths.

This morning at six I was reading St. John's passion and when Jesus was brought before Pilate, he was "asked about his disciples and his doctrine."

He certainly answered nothing about his disciples—he just said he had been preaching openly.

Our lives are open to all. We belong to a Kingdom not of this world, tho we are in it. May you be a constant reminder, a witness, of this other Kingdom, this glorious and beautiful Kingdom where we are willing and obedient and joyful subjects.

Remember St. Catherine of Siena said, "All the way to Heaven is heaven, because He said, 'I am the Way.'"

So may heaven be in your heart this day. We love you very much, and as for me, you have done so much to make me happy since you came to us, that mine is a very grateful love.

June 10, 1959

To Thomas Merton

Dorothy exchanged many letters with Thomas Merton, the Trappist monk, who became famous for his memoir, The Seven Storey Mountain, *and who in the 1960s contributed many articles to the* Catholic Worker *on peace and social issues. In her letters to him she often prayed for "perseverance"—both for him in his monastic vocation, and for herself.*

A very happy New Year to you and may you be faithful unto death.

My constant prayer is for final perseverance—to go on as I am trusting always the Lord Himself will take me by the hair of the head like Habakkuk and set me where he wants me.

December 23, 1959

An attack of arthritis and flu the last few weeks leaves me full of sloth. It is a good time to stay at the beach house where rain has driven people away. Aside from a disturbed family for whom I beg your prayers, and two ex-seamen puttering around fixing screens, I am alone. To be with eight people is to be alone at the CW. One of the men, Hugh Madden, was five years a brother at Gethsemani. "Disturbed" or a saint, who can tell? Both probably. . . .

Anyway, I am begging your prayers and be assured I pray for you as I hope you do for me. I am often full of fears about my final perseverance.

June 4, 1960

Every night we say the rosary and Compline in our little chapel over the barn, heavy with the smell of the cow downstairs (one can hear her chewing cud) and we have a bulletin board there with names of those who ask prayers. Yours is there. There are half a dozen old men, several earnest young ones, an old woman from the Bowery, a former teacher with one eye, a mother of an illegitimate child, and so on. We all say the rosary, only six remain for Compline. Do pray for us too. Your writing has reached many, many people and started them on their way. Be assured of that. It is the work God wants of you, no matter how much you want to run away from it. Like the Curé d'Ars. God bless you always.

October 10, 1960

I have a few friends who are always worrying about your leaving the monastery but from the letters from yours that I read I am sure you will hold fast. I myself pray for final perseverance, most fervently having seen one holy old priest suddenly elope with a parishioner. I feel that anything can happen to anybody at any time. But it does irritate me to hear these woeful predictions. As for your writing so much, I'm very glad you do. I am sure it is a gift of God and you are just as likely to dry up and not be able to write anything later on, so might as well do all you can now.

P.S. I am probably going to Rome April 16 with a group from Women Strike for Peace, who are foolishly expecting to get an audience [with the pope]. I told them it will probably be with 500 other people but a pilgrimage is a pilgrimage and if we can call attention to all things the Pope has been saying about peace, that in itself is good.

March 17, 1963

To a Peace Activist, regarding Marriage

Here, Dorothy wrote to a former editor of the Catholic Worker, *prominent in the peace movement, admonishing him over his plan to remarry without first obtaining an annulment.*

As you can well understand it is hard to write this. But I have been thinking about this for weeks and wondering what to do. And also what to say to you. In the chapel the other day I was so preoccupied with the problem that I made a few notes as to what to say and here they are.

First, when God asks great things of us, great sacrifices, He intends to do great things with us, though they will seem small, they will be most important. Who knows the power of the spirit. God's grace is more powerful than all the nuclear weapons that could possibly be accumulated.

Second, when we are asked to show our love for God, our desire for Him, when He asks us as Jesus asked Peter, "Lovest thou me?" we have to give proof of it. "Lovest thou me more than these, more than any human companionship, more than any human love?" It is not filth and ugliness, drugs and drink and perversion, he is asking us to prefer him to. He is asking us to prefer him to all beauty and loveliness. To all other love. He is giving us a chance to prove our faith, our hope, our charity. It is as hard and painful as Abraham's ordeal, when he thought he was asked to perform a human sacrifice and immolate his son. . . .

You are certainly going through the sorrowful mysteries. But if you don't go through them to the glorious, you will be a hollow man, and considered an opportunist and a fraud. I am putting it as strong as I am able, and hate doing it, but to me the Faith is the strongest thing in my life and I can never be grateful enough for the joy I have had for the gift of Faith, my Catholicism.

With love to you and begging you to forgive me for the pain I may have caused you.

Dorothy

March 3, 1967

To a Peace Activist, regarding His Doubts

Jim Douglass wrote me recently accusing me of suppressing part of your letter which we printed in the last or next to the last issue of the CW. I take it to mean the part when you tell me you no longer felt yourself a Catholic. I am trying to find that letter now in my heap of mail scattered over my desk and table, so that I can check how much I left out. I felt that I did not want to bring so personal a problem to our readers. You must know the deep unhappiness I felt and do feel. I have felt so many periods of dryness and heaviness and confusion myself, but also felt that I could only keep saying, "Lord, I believe, help thou my unbelief." And to try to keep my own deep sadness and discouragement from others. I think there are many periods of dryness, of searching and waiting for light in our lives. There is such a thing as deep spiritual fatigue, as well as physical. One can only "wait—and do nothing," as the psychiatrist in Eliot's *Cocktail Party* said.

Maybe you'd rather I did not write about these things in my correspondence to you. What I feel about the institutional church for instance. For me it is the place in the slum, in our neighborhood, where it is possible to be alone, to be silent, to wait on the Lord. The sacraments mean much to me. The daily bread we ask for is there. To sit in the presence of the Sun of Justice is healing, though I have to force myself to remain in fatigue and fullness and misery often. But the healing is there too. No matter how corrupt the church may become, it carries within it the seeds of its own regeneration. To read the lives of the saints has always helped me. We've had corrupt popes and bishops, down through the ages, but a St. Francis, a St. Benedict, a St. Vincent de Paul, a Charles de Foucauld will keep on reminding me of the primacy of the spiritual. Peter Maurin used to tell us to study history through the lives of the saints.

August 13, 1971

To Fritz Eichenberg, Quaker Artist

We both have our personal tragedies—our children's unhappinesses, but we have our work, a God-given work, a vocation which brings happiness, content, also. There are always two sides to the coin, joy and sadness. "In peace is my bitterness most bitter," is the old translation of a biblical text. I can understand it. But the Peace and Joy are there just the same. God can bring good out of evil. Ammon used to quote, "All things work for good to those who love God."

October 5, 1971

To a Young Woman in Distress

After spending the morning in a "good talk" with a young woman at the farm (as she noted in her diary), Dorothy "wrote her a long letter about suicide and abortion, prayer, salvation." This letter is notable for the references to her own abortion and two suicide attempts—events from her youth, long before her conversion, which she seldom, if ever, mentioned in writing or conversation. Despite her criticism of the climate of moral laxity, Dorothy (remembering her own troubled past) felt enormous compassion for the sufferings of the young.

Please forgive me for presuming to write you so personally—to intrude on you and your suffering, as I am doing, but I felt I had to—because I have gone thru so much the same suffering as you in the confusion of my youth and my search for love. I cannot help but feel deeply for you and for your mother, your family, because now I go through these sufferings over my grandchildren—one or another of them. In a way, to use old-fashioned language, I feel you are victim souls, bearing some of the agony the world is in, Vietnam, the Third World, "the misery of the needy and the groaning of the poor." But just the same it is a very real agony of our own, wanting human love, fulfillment, and one so easily sees all the imperfections of this love we seek, the inability of others ever to satisfy this need of ours, the constant failure of those nearest and dearest to understand, to respond.

But God has been so good to me, again and again, to make one know that when I cry out, even so feebly as calling, "God help me," He answers. "What have I on earth but Thee? What do I desire in Heaven beside thee? Hope thou in God," the Psalm goes on. "Hoping against hope," it says some place in Scripture. And "in peace is my bitterness most bitter"—such mysterious words—and yet it is hope, fragile hope—and a ray of peace, even if faint. I'm praying very hard for you this morning, because I myself have been thru much of what you have been through. Twice I tried to take my own life, and the dear Lord pulled me thru that darkness—I was rescued from that darkness. My sickness was physical too, since I had had an abortion with bad aftereffects, and in a way my sickness of mind was a penance I had to endure.

But God has been so good to me—I have known such joy in nature, and work—in writing, as you must get in your painting—in fulfilling myself, using my God-given love of beauty and desire to express myself. He has given me, over and over again, such joy and strength as He will surely give to you if you ask Him. "Taste and see that the Lord is sweet."

Again, I beg you to excuse me for seeming to intrude on you in this way. I know that just praying for you would have been enough. But we are human and must have human contact if only thru pen and paper. I love you, because you remind me of my own youth, and of my one child and my grandchildren. I will keep on praying for your healing, writing your name down in my little book of prayers which I have by my bedside at home. May love grow in your heart, and help you to express this love in joy and peace.

February 6, 1973

TO HERSELF

A Rule of Life

If you *are* discouraged, everyone would relapse into a state of discouragement and hopeless anger at circumstances and everyone else. And if you are not discouraged, everyone tries to make you be and are angry because you are not. It is hard to know what tack to take. The only thing is to be oblivious, as Peter is, and go right on and on. . . .

I am afraid my indignation at Peter's ideas being slighted had an element of self-love and pride in it, but just the same, there is ground for indignation. The crowd at the office get to Mass every morning, and are translating their spirituality into the natural order from morning to night. But it is true we are not "respectable"; we are criticized for our dress, our enthusiasm, and for the very works of mercy we are doing. Outside criticism is not so bad, but the criticism from within, the grumbling, the complaints, the insidious discontent spread around—these things are hard to bear.

However, the thing is to bear it patiently, to take it lightly, not to let it interfere with one's own work. The very fact that it is hard shows how much self-love and pride I have, what a deposit of meanness there is at the base of everything I do. I really am ashamed of myself, and shall try to do better. And I shall be happy too to think that God thinks I am strong enough to bear these trials, otherwise we would not be having them. Someone said we must beware when everything is going along smoothly. That is when there is no progress made.

In the evening there was a meeting in the office—Saturday night and all day Sunday, the meeting at Tom's, and as a visitor said, by that time they were all talked out. Fr. Furfey said a few more words about "spirituality" and to beware of "wordy ones," as St. Paul said; and I had a feeling he meant Peter, and probably me too, as I could be called a wordy one.

Oh dear, I am reminded of St. Teresa who said, "The devil sends me so offensive a bad spirit of temper that at times I think I could eat people up."

I am glad that she felt that way too. St. Thomas said that there is no sin in having a righteous wrath provided there is no undue desire for revenge.

I am afraid I am very stiff-necked. I shall read the Office and go to sleep. But first to concoct a rule for the coming year. It is a thing about which I have been meditating for quite some time—for two months to be exact.

I read in Tanqueray [*The Spiritual Life*] while on the trip that a rule of life was necessary for all, lay as [well as] cleric. So I resolved then to be more careful not to omit certain devotions that I let myself off from on account of my irregular life and fatigue. After all when I have been working from seven until twelve at night, or traveling fifteen hours by bus, I can realize all the more these words, "Can you not watch with me one hour?" That I have resolved is to be my motto for the coming year, in order to foster recollection.

December 31, 1935, *The Duty of Delight*

Reminders

I should know by this time that just because I *feel* that everything is useless and going to pieces and badly done and futile, it is not really that way at all. Everything is all right. It is in the hands of God. Let us abandon everything to Divine Providence.

And I must remember, too, that often beautiful scenery or a perfect symphony leaves me cold and dreary. There is nothing the matter with either the scenery or the music—it is myself. I have endured other miseries cheerfully at times. So I must be calm, patient, enduring and meditate on the gifts of the Holy Spirit.

I am writing this for my consolation and courage some future day when God sees fit and thinks me strong enough to bear longer, continued crosses.

It is to remind myself so that maybe I will be stronger.

House of Hospitality

A Lifetime Job

Oh yes, my dear comrades and fellow workers, I see only too clearly how bad things are with us all, how bad you all are, and how bad a leader I am. I see it only too often and only too clearly. It is because I see it so clearly that I must lift up my head and keep in sight the aims we must always hold before us. Must see the large and generous picture of the new social order wherein justice dwelleth. I must hold always in mind the new earth where God's Will will be done as it is in heaven. I must hold it in mind for my own courage and for yours. . . .

Even the best of human love is filled with self-seeking. To work to increase our love for God and for our fellow man (and the two must go hand in hand), this is a lifetime job. We are never going to be finished.

Love and ever more love is the only solution to every

problem that comes up. If we love each other enough, we will bear with each other's faults and burdens. If we love enough, we are going to light that fire in the hearts of others. And it is love that will burn out the sins and hatred that sadden us. It is love that will make us want to do great things for each other. No sacrifice and no suffering will then seem too much.

Yes, I see only too clearly how bad people are. I wish I did not see it so. It is my own sins that give me such clarity. If I did not bear the scars of so many sins to dim my sight and dull my capacity for love and joy, then I would see Christ more clearly in you all.

I cannot worry much about your sins and miseries when I have so many of my own. I can only love you all, poor fellow travelers, fellow sufferers. I do not want to add one least straw to the burden you already carry. My prayer from day to day is that God will so enlarge my heart that I will see you all, and live with you all, in His love.

House of Hospitality

A Time of Waiting

Advent is a time of waiting, of expectation, of silence. Waiting for our Lord to be born. A pregnant woman is so happy, so content. She lives in such a garment of silence, and it is as though she were listening to hear the stir of life within her. One always hears that stirring compared to the rustling of a bird in the hand. But the intentness with which one awaits such stirring is like nothing so much as a blanket of silence.

Be still. Did I hear something?

Be still and see that I am God.

In silence we hear so much that is beautiful. The other day I saw a young mother who said, "The happiest hour of the day is that early morning hour when I lie and listen to the baby practicing sounds and words. She has such a gentle little voice."

St. James says, "If any man offend not in word, the same is a perfect man." And how much more women need this gift of silence. It is something to be prayed for. Our Lady certainly had it. How little of her there is in the Gospel, and yet all generations have called her blessed. . . .

Many people think an examination of conscience is a morbid affair. Péguy has some verses which Donald Gallagher read to me once in the St. Louis House of Hospitality. They were about examination of conscience. There is a place for it, he said, at the beginning of the Mass. "I have sinned in thought, word, and deed, through my fault, through my fault, through my most grievous fault." But after you get done with it, don't go on brooding about it; don't keep thinking of it. You wipe your feet at the door of the church as you go in, and you do not keep contemplating your dirty feet.

Here is my examination at the beginning of Advent, at the beginning of a new year. Lack of charity, criticism of superiors, of neighbors, of friends and enemies. Idle talk, impatience, lack of self-control and mortification towards self, and of love towards others. Pride and presumption. (It is good to have visitors—one's faults stand out in the company of others.) Self-will, desire not to be corrected, to have one's own way. The desire in turn to correct others, impatience in thought and speech.

The remedy is recollection and silence. Meanness about giving time to others and wasting it myself. Constant desire for comfort. First impulse is always to make myself comfortable. If cold, to put on warmth; if hot, to become cool; if hungry, to eat; and what one likes—always the first thought is of one's own comfort. It is hard for a woman to be indifferent about little material things. She is a homemaker, a cook;

she likes to do material things. So let her do them *for others*, always. Woman's job is to love. Enlarge Thou my heart, Lord, that Thou mayest enter in.

December 1948, *On Pilgrimage*

Often I am tempted to depression, thinking that I have scarcely begun to live a spiritual life, even to live the way we all profess to, that of voluntary poverty and manual labor. It is a great cleanser of conscience, this living in community, with so many poor and suffering. That harsh saying, "You love God as much as the one you love the least," often comes to mind. But, just to say over and over again that one prayer, the *Our Father*, is to revive, to return to a sense of joy. "The worst malady of all is sadness," caused by lack of trust in the Lord and the desire to impose our own will on Him. Pope John wrote this in one of his letters to his family. In another place, there is this—"I repeat: to know how to say the *Our Father*, and to know how to put it into practice, this is the perfection of the Christian life."

September 1975

Wait and Do Nothing

When I was saying the Our Father and the Hail Mary this morning, it suddenly occurred to me how good it was to end our prayer to Mary with "now and at the hour of our death." I don't think I had ever realized how often we pray for the hour of our death, that it would be a good one. It is good, certainly, to have a long period of "ill health" . . . nothing specific, mild but frightening pains in the heart, and sickness, ebb-tide, ebbing of life, and then some days of strength and creativity.

"Wait and do nothing." This is the line my sister and I are fond of quoting to each other. We had seen T.S. Eliot's

The Cocktail Party together, and brought home with us that motto. I have never read the play, but that still sounds like a very good motto to me. How wonderful to be surrounded by loving kindness. Tulips, a rose, a picture, food. Tender, loving care! We all need it, sick or well.

June 1977

9

THE DUTY OF DELIGHT

Dorothy Day's life was marked by many dramatic events, shaped by her response to the great events and social movements of history. And yet, as is the case for most people, her life was largely spent in the uneventful business of daily life. Her diaries, published as The Duty of Delight, document some of this everyday life. The title came from a phrase she borrowed from the English critic John Ruskin; it appeared frequently within her diaries, often following a recital of drudgery or disappointment. It served as a reminder to find God in all things—the sorrows of daily life as well as the moments of joy.

Yet within this chronicle there is an underlying thread—an effort to read and reflect on her own life, her fluctuating moods, and the challenges of life in a house of hospitality in relation to her underlying quest for God. "On Pilgrimage" was the title Dorothy chose for her long-running column in the paper. More than just a chronicle of events and of her endless travels, it reflected her approach to life as a kind of pilgrimage, a journey defined by its ultimate goal.

In the following selections, drawn from her diaries, we see how Dorothy took note of her own "sins and shortcomings" as well as the presence of grace in her daily life. Her spirituality could well be understood as an echo of the famous words of St. Richard of

Chichester (d. 1253), who prayed to Christ for three things: "To see Thee more clearly, to love Thee more dearly, to follow Thee more nearly, day by day."

May 19, 1934

Such magnificent weather and today I have been feeling very happy. God rewards us for so little effort. Just a resolute turning to Him of our wills.

March 23, 1934

RESOLUTIONS: A sincere repentance for my sins—the result of turning my eyes inward on myself, instead of regarding the faults of others—this is what is most necessary for me. And having come to this conclusion matters straighten themselves out. When people fasten themselves to you with an emotional friendship it is hard, though. One is driven to a slightly strained reserve and the atmosphere is not a natural one.

September 22, 1934

Overcast, drizzling, warm. "The ear is not content with hearing nor the eye with seeing." I'm thinking of this because I'm listening to the Symphonic Hour on the radio—Brahms's 1st Symphony—and enjoying it very much, though Margaret bothers me with remarks about there being no butter, Tom asks for stencils, the baby frets, etc. Even so I enjoy it. But we cannot depend on our senses at all for enjoyment. What gives us keen enjoyment one day we listen to with indifference the next, the beauties of the beach arouse us to thanksgiving and exultation at one time and at another leave us lonely and miserable. "It is vanity to mind this present life, and not to look forward unto those things which are to come."

It is hard for me to look forward or to have any conception of future happiness. Sometimes I am afraid of this being lack of faith. On the other hand it makes it easier for me to live in the present moment as Caussade advises, and, let us hope, adds to the merit of endurance.

Hardships to offer up. Going to bed at night with the foul smell of unwashed bodies in my nostrils. Lack of privacy. But Christ was born in a stable and a stable is apt to be unclean and odorous. If the Blessed Mother could endure it, why not I? Also, Christ had no place to lay His head in the years of His public life. The birds of the air have their nests and the foxes their holes but the Son of Man has no place to lay His head.

October 25, 1934

I am constantly humiliated by my own imperfections and at my halting progress. Perhaps I deceive myself here too and excuse my lack of recollection. But I do know how small I am and how little I can do and I beg You, Lord, to help me for I cannot help myself. Touch my heart and help me to be ever mindful of Thee.

February 19, 1935

As I sit I am weeping—I have been torn recently by people, by things that happen. Surely we are, here in our community, made up of poor lost ones, the abandoned ones, the sick, the crazed, and the solitary human beings whom Christ so loved and in whom I see, with a terrible anguish, the body of this death. And out in the streets, wandering somewhere, is Mr. Minas, solitary among a multitude, surrounded by us all day long, but not one of us save in his humanity, denying, not knowing—yet clinging to some dream, some ideal of beauty which he tries to express in his poetry which no one but he can read.

Catherine is tossing in her bed, unable to sleep what with the wailing of cats in the backyard who act as though all the devils were in them—Catherine, too, with the misery of her illness hanging over her, with the uncertainty, the pain and nerve-racking treatments she undergoes.

I have seen too much of suffering recently what with visiting the girl who is in Woonsocket that Father Michael sent me to visit, who suffers in her skeleton body the torments Christ suffered. I cannot write about her—it is impossible to talk about these supernatural manifestations which are beyond my comprehension.

New Year, 1935
Some resolutions aside from Morning Prayer, reading the Office, saying the rosary daily:

I do plenty of spiritual reading to refresh myself and to encourage myself so I don't have to remind myself of that.

The thing to remember is not to read so much or talk so much about God, but to talk to God.

To practice the presence of God.

A nightly examination as to this role and not just about faults.

To be gentle and charitable in thought, word, and deed.

August 18, 1936
Low in mind all day, full of tears . . . I feel bitterly oppressed, yet confirmed in my conviction that we have to emphasize personal responsibility at all costs. It is most certainly at the price of bitter suffering for myself. For I am just in the position of a dictator trying to legislate himself out of existence. . . .

Since I got back from Pittsburgh I have had this completely alone feeling. A temptation of the devil, doubtless, and to succumb to it is a lack of faith and hope. There is nothing to do but bear it, but my heart is as heavy as lead, and my mind dull and uninspired. A time when the memory and understanding fail one completely and only the will remains, so that I feel hard and rigid, and at the same time ready to sit like a soft fool and weep my eyes out. . . . Never before have I had such a complete sense of failure.

May 8, 1937. St. Elizabeth Rectory, Chicago

What with being sick this week, felt very low tonight. Read, prayed, wept, and then thought—why do we expect any happiness? God wills for us the present moment. We must take it with a joyful will at least. Never let our moods affect others. Hide any sadness. We are suffering sadness and fatigue just because our will is painfully struggling. Our Lord must teach me, I cannot learn by myself to give up my will completely, to accept the present moment, to live in the presence of God. I should be happy that this struggle is going on, that I am not content. A paradox. I was just reading over the last pages herein for my help. It serves to convince me that nothing depends on me, I can do nothing. Moods, discouragement, bickerings pass and the work proceeds, the influence is far-reaching.

August 6, 1937

Love is a matter of the will . . . when it isn't just a biological urge that beclouds every other issue. If you will to love someone (even the most repulsive and wicked) and try to serve him as an expression of that love—then you soon come to *feel* love. And God will hear your prayer. "Enlarge Thou my heart that Thou mayest enter in!" You can pray the same way, that your heart may be enlarged to love again.

June 29, 1938

Meditation on the bus. Rainy and cold. Thinking gloomily of the sins and shortcomings of others, it suddenly came to me to remember my own offenses, just as heinous as those of others. If I concern myself with my own sins and lament them, if I remember my own failures and lapses, I will not be resentful of others. This was most cheering and lifted the load of gloom from my mind. It makes one unhappy to judge people and happy to love them.

July 17, 1938

Our greatest need is mutual charity, love, and loyalty to each other. It is the only way to solve problems, get cooperation, and have peace. To see the good in our neighbor, and develop it. To forgive and not to judge. Never to speak ill of one another. . . .

My problem is not to become upset at people's discontent and criticism but to keep myself peaceful, kind, and patient. My great fault when one person is criticizing another is to point out their faults and that only makes things worse.

March 1, 1939

I do not have to retire to my room to pray. It is enough to get out and walk in the wilderness of the streets.

July 3, 1939

Warm, sunny. Great depression of spirits. Job is to hide it from others, to accept it as penance, reparation, and to pray constantly for an increase in my heart of the love of God and man.

July 8, 1939

About others' sins. Drunkenness and all the things which follow in its wake are so obviously ugly and monstrous, and mean such unhappiness for the poor sinner that it is all the more important that we do not judge or condemn. In the eyes of God the hidden subtle sins must be far worse. We must make every effort of will to love more and more—to hang on to each other with love. They should serve to show us the hideousness of our own sins so that we truly repent and abhor them.

January 17, 1940

We all see thru a glass darkly. Some see more clearly than others. Our joy in the work increases with our vision of the whole. Just as when a man uses his whole body he is in better health. Not just head or hand. Workers must be scholars and scholars workers, as Peter says.

Heaven is when we see God face to face, when we shall see Him as He is. Now it is only a glimpse, a suggestion of light, of joy, of unity, of completion. . . .

March 15, 1940

Bertha says I am gruff and indifferent to people (she means when I come off the platform or am meeting a mass of them at a time). She rightly points out we are trying to change people's attitudes, to create understanding, to combat class war. So I must learn to be more cordial to people and overcome that immense sense of weariness and even impatience when people, quite sincerely, tell me how they enjoy my books, how interested they are in my work. Miss Jordan told me I look at people as tho they were going to steal 5 minutes of my time! It makes me unhappy to give such an impression, I feel as tho I had failed people again and again, not only on trips, but at Mott St. I must do better, guard myself rigidly, control my fatigue, not mention it. But oh, it is so hard, I'll just have to work every day at it.

These hours on trains or bus are so precious—to be

alone for a short while, it is a complete relaxation, a joy. I am a weak and faulty vessel to be freighted with so valuable a message as cargo. I am an unprofitable servant and must begin over again right now to change myself. God help me.

July 6, 1940

My nights are always in sadness and desolation and it seems as tho as soon as I lie down I am on a rack of bitterness and pain. Then in the day I am again strong enough to make an act of faith and love and go on in peace and joy.

August 27, 1940

It always makes me feel selfish but I must confess my weakness that I cannot do without. Always when I come down to the farm there are so many problems, so much unrest which seems to center around me since everyone wishes me to settle something, that I need some time alone for prayer and reading so that I can attain some proper perspective and peace of spirit to deal with myself and others. I need to overcome a sense of my own impotence, my own failure, and an impatience at others that goes with it. I must remember not to judge myself, as St. Paul says. Such a sense of defeat comes from expecting too much of one's self, also from a sense of pride. More and more I realize how good God is to me to send me discouragements, failures, antagonisms.

The only way to proceed is to remember that God's ways are not our ways. To bear our own burdens, do our own work as best we can, and not fret because we cannot do more or do another's work. To be in that state of mind is to get nothing done.

July 19, 1943

For the last days I have felt a stronger determination, a resolution to spend more time in prayer and work. And suddenly there crystallized in my mind an idea that had been working there for some time, even for some years. I more or less expressed it when I talked of going off to be a "desert father." ...

I always felt God would indicate his will for me by some exterior act—by the paper being suppressed, by the Archbishop suggesting that I leave. Now it suddenly comes to me, Why do I not just hand the paper over to Peter and Arthur, Dave and Fr. Duffy, and leave? I no longer feel I can save my soul by this work; no, more, I am in danger of losing it. I am in danger of becoming like that woman in *Bleak House* who worked so hard for foreign missions and neglected her family. Or like that woman in *The Possessed*, the Governor's wife, who had a finger in every pie and felt important. St. Paul defines woman's place. Sister Peter Claver says woman's place is to love and to suffer.

What I want to do is get a job, in some hospital as wardmaid, get a room, preferably next door to a church; and there in the solitude of the city, living and working with the poor; to learn to pray, to work, to suffer, to be silent.

The world is too much with me in the Catholic Worker. The world is suffering and dying. I am not suffering and dying in the CW. I am writing and talking about it.

Of course I will not save my soul alone. Wherever we are we are with people. We drag them down, or pull them up. Or we get dragged down or pulled up. And in recognition of this latter fact, I recognize also the need for aids and counsel in the path to God.

That is why as soon as possible I will try to organize days of recollection—primarily for myself. I will not be able to stand the impact of the world otherwise. Primarily for myself. But that will mean others—how many, who can tell? And later, retreats! We can do nothing today without saints; big ones and little ones. The only weapons we will develop will be those of prayer and penance. And the world will leave us alone, saying—after all, they are not doing anything. Just a bunch of smug fools praying. We will not be as tormented by its scorn as we are by the praise of the world for works of mercy, houses of hospitality, and farming communes. They are necessary—they are the results of the work we are beginning. It is only by the grace of God they have sprung up and prospered.

But we need thousands of hospices after the war—thousands of refuges, thousands of "farming communes." And we need saints to start them and to operate them.

Hence this new move. Hence this running away, to seek a hidden life.

I have always been so sure I was right, that I was being led by God—that is, in the main outlines of my life—that I confidently expected Him to show His will by external events.

And I looked for some unmistakable sign. I disregarded all the little signs. I begin now to see them and with such clearness that I have to beg not to be shown too much, for fear I cannot bear it.

I need strength to do what I have to do—strength and joy and peace and vision.

Lord, that I may see! That prayer is certainly answered most overwhelmingly on this retreat. It shows one has to make at least three retreats before you slough off the thick skin, so as to become sensitive enough to feel the breath of his inspirations.

August 8, 1946

My love of peace and quiet inclines me always to want to do nothing. This drag to take my ease is like the pull of gravity. Will it always be so? My first impulse is always to say *no.* God forgive me for this unwillingness which pollutes all my actions.

March 25, 1950

At 1:00 a man and woman came bringing a drunken woman in and I was very harsh in not taking her. As Tom said, before dawn came, I had denied our Lord in her. I felt very guilty—more for my manner than for doing it, as we could not have all the other women in the house disturbed.

June 16, 1951

Anger is momentary. Some people will never apologize tho they may feel sorry. Everything is bottled up inside and it is unseemly, to say the least, to be always trying to pry people open, to make them open (as I consider myself to be, for instance). . . . My problem is to try and be gentle and kind to *all.* Even, equable, never startling and saddening people by changes of mood. Lifting an atmosphere instead of lowering it. . . . I have a hard enough job to curb the anger in my own heart which I sometimes even wake up with, go to sleep with—a giant to strive with, an ugliness, a sorrow to me—a mighty struggle to love. As long as there is any resentment, bitterness, lack of love in my own heart I am powerless. God must help me. . . . The talk with Jane was good because it made me see my own faults, flippancy, criticalness, gibing attitude, lack of respect and love for others.

January 13, 1952

O God, give me the grace ever to alleviate the crosses of those around me, never to add to them.

Our house will hold just so many, we can feed just so many, and after that we must say no. It makes us realize how little we can do. It is a constant grief, and a humbling of our pride. One woman said to me, "If I knew how sensitive you were, I would not have told you my troubles." So we cannot show how we suffer with them either. We make them feel we are adding to the sum total of suffering instead of lightening it.

August 8, 1952
I fail people daily, God help me, when they come to me for aid and sympathy. There are too many of them, whichever way I turn. It is not that I can do anything. I must always disappoint them and arouse their bitterness, especially when it is material things they want. But I deny them the Christ in me when I do not show them tenderness, love. God forgive me, and make up to them for it.

August 20, 1952
Dear God—I'll try as an exercise, to write my meditations since I am sidetracked in your presence. I find myself saying over and over with my lips—Oh God, O Lord, make haste to help me. O Lord Jesus, have mercy, with every breath I draw. But how much of it is surface, and how much is deep? You know. Only You. . . . I believe You are a personal God, and hear me when I speak, even my trivial petty speech. So I will tell You personally over and over I love You, I adore You, I worship You. Make me mean it in my life. Make me show it by my choices. Make me show it from my waking thought to my sleeping.

September 29, 1954
Little Flower begged God to let her always see *reality*. Things as they *really* were, so her love would be true and real.

Bad angels can attack us thru our imagination. But they cannot reach our will—our intellect.

June 13, 1958
Opportunities to grow in spiritual life—parakeet screaming while symphony is on radio. Mice; coughing; fragments of food; cockroaches; chatter.

December 16, 1958

Yesterday morning woke with the most certain understanding that all in this life is surely a preparation for the next, a practice, a study, to pass our exams. Also a sense of the real work of that hour of prayer. That feat of endurance, that hour in the desert, that hour of suffering that the Little Sisters make that our Lord can transform so easily into joy.

February 12, 1959

It is hard to convince anyone, priest or people, that Charity must forgive seventy times seven, and that we must not judge. The bitterness with which people regard the poor and down-and-out. Drink, profligate living, laziness, everything is suspected. They help them once, the man who comes to the door, but they come back! They want more help. "Where will it end? Can I accomplish anything? Aren't there poorer people whom I should be helping?" These are the questions they ask themselves, which paralyzes all charity, chills it, stops all good work. If we start in by admitting that what we can do is very small—a drop in the bucket—and try to do that very well, it is a beginning and really a great deal.

Here I am, 61 years old, and I can remember three incidents of people with very sweet expressions, happy smiles, welcoming looks, among all my casual encounters, who quite warmed my heart for the rest of the day. People who are in our position, where many calls are made on them, are apt to get a guarded expression, a suspicious look, or even an angry look when they feel frustrated at not being able to help as they wish. Oh! to start out each day and greet each encounter with open arms—a message from our dear Lord, a friend of His, someone He sent, His guest, not ours.

June 7, 1960

I felt impelled to write to Karl [Stern] about my troubles and suddenly thought—they have enough troubles. Why add to their burden?

The other day when writing my article and appeal I threw away my article telling of all our troubles and thought "this is not what our readers want—to be tortured with tales of broken families, men beating their wives and children, etc."

I will write happily of June and its beauties. Of course if you do this you get a double share of complaints from all around you who try to make you see how bad everything is. Still you cannot help but help others by your own repose and joy if you try to maintain it.

February 24, 1961

Today I thought of a title for my book, "The Duty of Delight," as a sequel to "The Long Loneliness." I was thinking, how as one gets older, we are tempted to sadness, knowing life as it is here on earth, the suffering, the Cross. And how we must overcome it daily, growing in love, and the joy which goes with loving.

July 2, 1963

Today the atmosphere very heavy. Rain threatens. So often one is overcome with a tragic sense of the meaninglessness of our lives—patience, patience, and the very word means suffering. Endurance, perseverance, sacrament of the present moment, the sacrament of duty. One must keep on reassuring oneself of these things. And repeat acts of faith. "Lord, I believe, help thou my unbelief." We are placed here; why? To know Him, and so love Him, serve Him, by serving others and so attain to eternal life and joy, understanding, etc.

January 1966

"Eye hath not seen, nor ear heard what God hath prepared for those who love Him." But do I love Him? The only test is am I willing to sacrifice present happiness and present love for Him? I have done it once, and thereby kept them. The thing is, one must keep doing it, day after day, beginning over and over, to count all things but dross compared to the life of the spirit which alone is able to bring joy, overcome fear—"Love casts out fear." "I know that my redeemer liveth, and in my flesh I shall see God my Savior . . . I believe—help Thou my unbelief." Most of the time I am as sure of these things as I am of my own life. And as for those periods of desert and doubt, there is so much in the line of inescapable duty that one can work one's way thru them.

God respects man and gives him the tremendous gift of freedom, not wishing the love of a slave. He allows man even to sin, tho he knows man will turn as to a parent and blame Him, "Why am I born? Why did He let this happen to me?" I started thinking of this yesterday, that if God respects man and his freedom, so must I respect Him, by not judging—by leaving him to be God, who alone knows and understands him, whom He has created. We must not judge, but always try to love.

June 16, 1966

Woke this a.m. with the feeling very strong—I belong to Someone to whom I owe devotion. Recalled early love and that joyous sense of being not my own, but of belonging to someone who loved me completely.

January 6, Epiphany 1967

Wept all morning over state of world and the house. . . . People talk so much about the meaning of life and the work is to grow in love, love of God our destination, and love of neighbor, our first step, our continuing step, our right road in that direction. Love means answering the mail that comes in—and there is a fearful amount of it. That person in the hospital, that person suffering a breakdown of nerves, the person lonely, far-off, watching for the mailman each day. It means loving attention to those around us, the youngest and the oldest (the drunk and the sober).

Easter Sunday, April 14, 1968

Always when I awaken in the morning it is to a half-dead condition, a groaning in every bone, a lifelessness, a foretaste of death, a sense of "quiet terror," which hangs over us all. A sense of the futility of life and the worthlessness of all our efforts. It is, as one of our retreat masters said, as tho we rowed a fragile bark at the head of Niagara Falls and all our efforts are to keep from going over into the chasm below.

I turn desperately to prayer. "O God make haste to help me. Take not Thy Holy Spirit from me." And there is always Matins or Lauds, those magnificent psalms, the official prayer of the church, prayers which thousands, tens of thousands are saying each morning all over the world. And I am saved.

This consciousness of salvation comes to me afresh each day. I am turned around, away from the contemplation of the world of sin and death to the reality of God, our loving Father, who so loved us he gave us his son, Sun of Justice, who became sin for us, sharing our human condition, bore the penalty, our death, and showed us the resurrection. He overcame it.

Thru this turning around, "all the way to heaven is heaven" to me, as St. Catherine of Siena said. The sun has risen, the air is warmed, the birds are singing outside and I go outside to sit by the dead-calm river, which flows by, the tide carrying bits of driftwood, the only thing indicative of motion, of progress toward the sea.

And from quiet terror, I go on to quiet joy at God's goodness and love in giving us Jesus to show us how to love. The testimony of our hearts shows us the truth. We experience, no matter how briefly, the sense of salvation He won for us. Assassinations, wars, the lying and treachery of man, even the best of men, what with his capacity for evil, fades out in such blinding flashes of light.

The saints, who renounced themselves, who did penance, who starved themselves with fasting, who scourged themselves, kept vigil, were burnt by heat and paralyzed by cold but felt only joy at such sharing of Jesus' Passion.

And what woman is there who does not and would not willingly suffer for love of man and love of the child which comes into this world with cries and with blood.

June 18, 1970

I do believe in a personal God, because I too have had revelations, answers to my questions, to my prayers, and if the answer fails to come, which is usually the case because God wants us to work out our own salvation, I have that assurance God gave St. Paul and he passed on to us, "My grace is sufficient for you."

And what is grace? Participation in the divine life. And that participation means for me light and understanding and conviction, of course only occasionally, but strong enough to carry me along, to lift me up out of depression, discouragement, uncertainty, doubt. . . .

My mother used to say, "When you are in the dumps, clean house, take a bath, dress up, go downtown and window-shop." Everything passes, St. Teresa of Avila says.

March 6, 1973
Strange experience of being penetrated by God.

April 27, 1973
To *be* is good. I am grateful for life, to *be* in this world, frightful though it is today with wars spreading and expanding.

October 23 1976
"I have sinned exceedingly in my youth," Tolstoy said in a conversation with Gorki. I remember that often in my prayers for the young, and whenever people speak of my *Long Loneliness* as an autobiography. It is rather a story of a conversion. Aside from drug addiction, I committed all the sins young people commit today. I am glad we repeat the Confiteor every day at Mass. I am glad I know so many prayers by rote such as the Memorare and the Act of Contrition. They are no more meaningless than a beautiful poem is.

May 29, Pentecost, 1977
Woke up with great feelings of joy and gratitude to God for his great gifts of the Holy Spirit.

January 23, 1978
Sun on tree. "The world will be saved by beauty."

October 27, 1978
At exactly 8:05 a.m. the morning sun gilded the building across the street creeping from grey over to red brick one. A lovely sight. Pigeons fly from the roofs—the ailanthus tree stirs in the cold east wind, the sky is a cloudless blue—and now one side of the ailanthus tree which reaches the third

floor of the once-luxury tenements is all gilded, and the sun spreads rapidly around it. Young people are on their way to work but children not yet on their way to school. . . .

My tree is now radiant with sun.

November 1, 1978
Notes on last two days show my grievances! Must cultivate holy indifference.

January 6, 1979
Woke up with two lines haunting me, "Duty of delight." And "Joyous I lay waste the day."

February 5, 1979
I woke up this morning with a tune running thru my head— "He has the whole world in His hands, He has the whole wide world, in His hands." So why worry? Why lament? "Rejoice," the Psalmist writes, "and again I say Rejoice!"

10

MAKING PEACE

Dorothy's commitment to gospel nonviolence was expressed very early in the life of the Catholic Worker. The first occasion was in response to the Spanish Civil War, a war regarded by most of her fellow Catholics as virtually a holy war against godless atheism. For Dorothy this was a radical test of belief in the teachings of Christ. Christ preached a message of love that extended even to our enemies—not to the point of reason, prudence, or personal safety, but unreasonably, foolishly, unto the Cross. In an era of ever-widening violence, she spoke of the Sermon on the Mount as the "manifesto" of the Catholic Worker and called on Christians to undertake a "disarmament of the heart."

The Use of Force

Christ our Lord came and took upon Himself our humanity. He became the Son of Man. He suffered hunger and thirst and hard toil and temptation. All power was His but He wished the free love and service of men. He did not force anyone to believe. St. Paul talks of the liberty of Christ. He did not coerce anyone. He emptied Himself and became a servant. He showed the way to true leadership by coming to minister, not to be ministered unto. He set the example and we are supposed to imitate Him. We are taught that His kingdom was not of this earth. He did not need pomp and circumstance to prove Himself the Son of God.

His were hard sayings, so that even His own followers did not know what he was saying, did not understand
Him. It was not until after He died on the Cross, it was not
until He had suffered utter defeat, it would seem, and they
thought their cause was lost entirely; it was not until they
had persevered and prayed with all the fervor and desperation of their poor loving hearts, that they were enlightened
by the Holy Spirit and knew the truth with a strength that
enabled them to suffer defeat and martyrdom in their turn.
They knew then that not by force of arms, by the bullet or
the ballot, they would conquer. They knew and were ready
to suffer defeat—to show that great love which enabled them
to lay down their lives for their friends.

And now the whole world is turning to "force" to conquer. Fascist and Communist alike believe that only by
the shedding of blood can they achieve victory. Catholics,
too, believe that suffering and the shedding of blood "must
needs be" as Our Lord said to the disciples at Emmaus. But
their teaching, their hard saying is, that they must be willing to shed every drop of their own blood, and not take
the blood of their brothers. They are willing to die for their
faith, believing that the blood of martyrs is the seed of the
Church.

Our Lord said, "Destroy this temple and in three days
I will raise it up." And do not His words apply not only to
Him as Head of his Church but to His members? How can
the Head be separated from the members? The Catholic
Church cannot be destroyed in Spain or in Mexico. But we
do not believe that force of arms can save it. We believe that
if Our Lord were alive today he would say as He said to
St. Peter, "Put up thy sword."

Christians when they are seeking to defend their faith
by arms, by force and violence, are like those who said to

our Lord, "Come down from the Cross. If you are the Son of God, save yourself."

But Christ did not come down from the Cross. He drank to the last drop the agony of His suffering and was not part of the agony the hopelessness, the unbelief of His own disciples.

Christ is being crucified today, every day. Shall we ask Him with the unbelieving world to come down from the Cross? Or shall we joyfully, as His brothers, "complete the sufferings of Christ"? . . .

Prince of Peace, Christ our King, Christ our Brother, Christ the Son of Man, have mercy on us and give us the courage to suffer. Help us to make ourselves "a spectacle to the world and to angels and to men." Help your priests and people in Spain to share in your suffering, and in seeming defeat, giving up their lives, without doubt there will be those like the centurion, standing at the foot of the Cross who will say, "Indeed these men are the sons of God."

November 1936

Disarming Hearts

Today the whole world is in the midst of a revolution. We are living through it now—all of us. History will record this time as a time of world revolution. And frankly, we are calling for Saints. The Holy Father in his call for Catholic Action, for the lay apostolate, is calling for Saints. We must prepare now for martyrdom—otherwise we will not be ready. Who of us if he were attacked now would not react quickly and humanly against such attack? Would we love our brother who strikes us? Of all at the Catholic Worker how many would not instinctively defend himself with any forceful means in his power? We must prepare. We must prepare now. There must be a disarmament of the heart.

Yes, wars will go on. We are living in a world where even "Nature itself travaileth and groaneth" due to the Fall. But we cannot sit back and say "human nature being what it is, you cannot get a man to overcome their adversary by love."

We are afraid of the word love and yet love is stronger than death, stronger than hatred.

If we do not, as the press, emphasize the law of love, we betray our trust, our vocation. We must stand opposed to the use of force.

St. Paul, burning with zeal, persecuted the church. But he was converted.

Again and again in the history of the church, the conquered overcome the conquerors.

We are not talking of passive resistance. Love and prayer are not passive but a most active glowing force.

And we ask with grief who are they amongst us who pray with faith and with love, and so powerfully that they can move the mountains of hatred that stand in our path. The soul needs exercise as well as the body and if we do not exercise our soul in prayer now, we will be puny and ineffectual in the trials that await us.

We are praying for the Spanish people—all of them our brothers in Christ—all of them Temples of the Holy Ghost, all of them members or potential members of the Mystical Body of Christ.

And we add daily to this prayer for peace: "Lord, teach us to pray: 'Lord I believe, help Thou my unbelief.'" "Lord, take away my heart of stone and give me a heart of flesh."

September 1938

The Second World War:
"Our Manifesto Is the Sermon on the Mount"

Our Country Passes from Undeclared War to Declared War; We Continue Our Christian Pacifist Stand

DEAR FELLOW WORKERS IN CHRIST:
Lord God, merciful God, our Father, shall we keep silent, or shall we speak? And if we speak, what shall we say?

I am sitting here in the church on Mott Street writing this in your presence. Out on the streets it is quiet, but you are there too, in the Chinese, in the Italians, these neighbors we love. We love them because they are our brothers, as Christ is our Brother and God our Father.

But we have forgotten so much. We have all forgotten. And how can we know unless you tell us. "For whoever calls upon the name of the Lord shall be saved." How then are they to call upon Him in whom they have not believed? But how are they to believe Him whom they have not heard? And how are they to hear, if no one preaches? And how are men to preach unless they be sent? As it is written, "How beautiful are the feet of those who preach the gospel of peace." (Romans X)

Seventy-five thousand *Catholic Workers* go out every month. What shall we print? We can print still what the Holy Father is saying, when he speaks of total war, of mitigating the horrors of war, when he speaks of cities of refuge, of feeding Europe. . . .

We will print the words of Christ who is with us always, even to the end of the world. "Love your enemies, do good to those who hate you, and pray for those who persecute and calumniate you, so that you may be children of your

Father in heaven, who makes His sun to rise on the good and the evil, and sends rain on the just and unjust."

We are at war, a declared war, with Japan, Germany and Italy. But still we can repeat Christ's words, each day, holding them close in our hearts, each month printing them in the paper. In times past, Europe has been a battlefield. But let us remember St. Francis, who spoke of peace and we will remind our readers of him, too, so they will not forget.

In *The Catholic Worker* we will quote our Pope, our saints, our priests. We will go on printing the articles which remind us today that we are all "called to be saints," that we are other Christs, reminding us of the priesthood of the laity.

We are still pacifists. Our manifesto is the Sermon on the Mount, which means that we will try to be peacemakers. Speaking for many of our conscientious objectors, we will not participate in armed warfare or in making munitions, or by buying government bonds to prosecute the war, or in urging others to these efforts.

But neither will we be carping in our criticism. We love our country and we love our President. We have been the only country in the world where men of all nations have taken refuge from oppression. We recognize that while in the order of intention we have tried to stand for peace, for love of our brother, in the order of execution we have failed as Americans in living up to our principles.

We will try daily, hourly, to pray for an end to the war, such an end, to quote Father Orchard, "as would manifest to all the world, that it was brought about by divine action, rather than by military might or diplomatic negotiation, which men and nations would then only attribute to their power or sagacity." . . .

Our works of mercy may take us into the midst of war. As editor of *The Catholic Worker*, I would urge our friends and associates to care for the sick and the wounded, to the growing of food for the hungry, to the continuance of all our works of mercy in our houses and on our farms. We understand, of course, that there is and that there will be great differences of opinion even among our own groups as to how much collaboration we can have with the government in times like these. There are differences more profound and there will be many continuing to work with us from necessity, or from choice, who do not agree with us as to our position on war, conscientious objection, etc. But we beg that there will be mutual charity and forbearance among us all.

Because of our refusal to assist in the prosecution of war and our insistence that our collaboration be one for peace, we may find ourselves in difficulties. But we trust in the generosity and understanding of our government and our friends, to permit us to continue, to use our paper to "preach Christ crucified."

May the Blessed Mary, Mother of love, of faith, of knowledge and of hope, pray for us.

January 1942

A Spectacle to the World

Beginning in 1955, Dorothy and other pacifists refused to cooperate with compulsory civil defense drills in New York City. She was repeatedly arrested and jailed for sentences ranging from five to thirty days.

We probably all experienced different things, the thirty of us who were arrested in City Hall Park at 2:05 p.m., June 15, for refusing to obey the Air Raid wardens and taking to shelter.

There were thirty of us piled in a police van meant to accommodate 10. Why did we do it? What did the Chancery office think of it all? Of these ten Catholics making a spectacle of themselves, "a spectacle to the world, to angels and to men."

To answer that question, we got out one long leaflet and one short statement to be read before the newsreel camera. My statement read:

> We make this demonstration, not only to voice our opposition to war, not only to refuse to participate in psychological warfare, which this air raid drill is, but also as an act of public penance for having been the first people in the world to drop the atom bomb, to make the hydrogen bomb. We are engaging only ourselves in this action, not the Church. We are acting as individual Catholics. Jacques Maritain, the French philosopher has written, "We are turning towards men, to speak and act among them, on the temporal plane, because, by our faith, by our baptism, by our confirmation, tiny as we are, we have the vocation of infusing into the world, wheresoever we are, the sap and savor of Christianity."

This was but a slight experience, this imprisonment, and our readers have no opportunity actually of visiting the prisoner, we realize that. We have got to pray. With love, there is no time, no space, nor bars.

July–August 1955

Visiting the Prisoner

When I think of the long sentences served by so many others in so many miscarriages of justice, when I think of the accumulation of prisons, outmoded and futile that dot the land of the free, I am not particularly interested in writing about my few days in jail last month. I am just glad that I served them, and am ready to serve again if there is another compulsory air raid drill next summer. It is a gesture perhaps, but a necessary one. Silence means consent, and we cannot consent to the militarization of our country without protest. Since we believe that the air raid drills are part of a calculated plan to inspire fear of the enemy instead of the love which Jesus Christ told us we should feel toward him we must protest these drills. It is an opportunity to show we mean what we write when we repeat over and over, that man is here on this earth, to love God and His brother.

It was good to have the opportunity to "visit the prisoner," which is one of the works of mercy, even for so brief a visit, by being a prisoner one's self.

February 1957

A Prayer for Peace

In 1965, during the final session of Vatican II, Dorothy traveled to Rome to join a group of women fasting and praying for ten days to encourage the Council fathers to issue a strong statement against nuclear war. Their prayers were answered in the statement in the Pastoral Constitution on the Church in the Modern World, "Any act of war aimed indiscriminately at the destruction of entire cities or extensive areas along with their population is a crime against God and man himself. It merits unequivocal and unhesitating condemnation."

Our prayer and our hope is that from the chair of Peter, from the College of Cardinals will come during this last session of the Council, a clear statement, "Put up thy sword," with the healing touch of Jesus in such a statement to the ears of those who, hearing, do not understand.

The apostles didn't take the sword, they cowered in fear instead and could scarcely believe that they saw Him again.

They were still asking Him about when the earthly kingdom would come despite His clear statement that His kingdom was not of this world which is a testing ground, a place of trial, a school of Christ, as St. Benedict had it.

But after the Holy Spirit enlightened the apostles they went to martyrdom, embraced the cross, laid down their own lives for their neighbors, in whom they were beginning to see Christ.

"Inasmuch as ye have done it unto one of the least of these my brethren you have done it unto me."

We long with all our hearts for such a statement from the Bishops, clear, uncompromising, courageous. We know that men in their weakness, like the apostles, will still take the sword, will still be denying Christ in their brother the Negro, the Vietnamese.

But the teaching of Jesus has indeed been answered again and again over the ages, from the apostles to the present day and again and again those called by the Holy Spirit and touched by grace have laid down their lives for the Faith that God is our Father and all men are our brothers.

"A new commandment I give unto you, that you love others as I have loved you," that is to the *laying down* of one's life. The commandment of love, which is binding on us all, in Old Testament and New, was finally heard by Peter, once the denier, and by Franz Jägerstätter [*an Austrian Catholic who was executed for refusing to serve in Hitler's army*]. And by how many others through the ages whose histories have never been written? Our God is a hidden God, and such stories are hidden too in the lives of the saints.

Christ is being martyred today in Vietnam, in Santo Domingo and in all places where men are taking to the sword in this world crisis. He will be crucified to the end of time. He is with us in His humanity until the end of time.

Unless we use the weapons of the spirit, denying ourselves and taking up our cross and following Jesus, dying with Him and rising with Him, men will go on fighting, and often from the highest motives, believing that they are fighting defensive wars for justice for others and in self-defense against present or future aggression. . . .

Without religious conversion there will be few Franz Jägerstätters to stand alone and leave wife and children and farm for conscience' sake. But as Jägerstätter said, it was God's grace that moved him—more powerful, we know, than any hydrogen bomb.

July–August 1965

"I Speak as One Who Is Old"

At a rally in Union Square on November 6, 1965, Dorothy joined veteran peacemaker A. J. Muste in supporting young men burning their draft cards in protest of the Vietnam War. Her speech was later reprinted in The Catholic Worker.

When Jesus walked this earth, True God and True man, and was talking to the multitudes, a woman in the crowd cried out, "Blessed is the womb that bore you and the breast that nourished you." And he answered her, "Yes, but rather, blessed are those who hear the word of God and keep it."

And the word of God is the new commandment he gave us—to love our enemies, to overcome evil with good, to love others as he loved us—that is, to lay down our lives for our brothers throughout the world, not to take the lives of men, women, and children, young and old, by bombs and napalm and all the other instruments of war.

Instead he spoke of the instruments of peace, to be practiced by all nations—to feed the hungry of the world—not to destroy their crops, not to spend billions on defense, which means instruments of destruction. He commanded us to feed the hungry, shelter the homeless, to save lives, not to destroy them, these precious lives for whom he willingly sacrificed his own.

I speak today as one who is old, and who must uphold and endorse the courage of the young who themselves are willing to give up their freedom. I speak as one who is old, and whose whole lifetime has seen the cruelty and hysteria of war in this last half century. But who has also seen, praise God, the emerging nations of Africa and Asia, and Latin America, achieving in many instances their own freedom through nonviolent struggles, side by side with violence. Our own country has, through tens of thousands of the Negro people, shown an example to the world of what a nonviolent struggle can achieve. This very struggle, begun by students, by the young, by the seemingly helpless, has led the way in vision, in courage, even in a martyrdom, which has been shared by the little children, in the struggle for full freedom and for human dignity, which means the right to health, education, and work which is a full development of man's God-given talents.

We have seen the works of man's genius and vision in the world today, in the conquering of space, in his struggle with plague and famine, and in each and every demonstration such as this one—there is evidence of his struggle against war.

I wish to place myself beside A. J. Muste speaking, if I am permitted, to show my solidarity of purpose with these young men, and to point out that we too are breaking the law, committing civil disobedience, in advocating and trying to encourage all those who are conscripted, to inform their conscience, to heed the still small voice, and to refuse to participate in the immorality of war. It is the most potent way to end war.

We too, by law, myself and all who signed the statement of conscience, should be arrested and we would esteem it an honor to share prison penalties with these others. I would like to conclude these few words with a prayer in the words of St. Francis, saint of poverty and peace, "O Lord, make me an instrument of your peace. Where there is hatred, let me sow love."

November 1965

11

A Revolution of the Heart

Among the basic principles of the Catholic Worker was the recognition of Christ in one's neighbors, especially the poor. That principle was the foundation supporting houses of hospitality for the practice of the Works of Mercy. This was joined by a second principle: the critique of a social order that gave rise to so much poverty and injustice. In joining the practice of charity with work for justice, Dorothy was in effect answering the question she had posed in her youth: "Where were the saints to change the social order, not just to minister to the slaves but to do away with slavery?" And yet there was a third principle. That was the commitment to point toward an alternative society, to show that another way of living was possible. Peter Maurin believed it was not enough to protest everything you were against. It was even more important to proclaim what you were for. That meant, first of all, trying to live by the values you were proclaiming. He wanted to build a society "where it was easier for people to be good"—a society organized around solidarity and community, rather than competition and individualism; on systematic generosity and hospitality, rather than greed and hostility. This alternative society could begin exactly where we were, today. It was expressed in voluntary poverty, in community, personalism, and nonviolence. Dorothy called it "a revolution of the heart."

THE REVOLUTION WE NEED

The greatest challenge of the day is: how to bring about a revolution of the heart, a revolution which has to start with each one of us. When we begin to take the lowest place, to wash the feet of others, to love our brothers with that burning love, that passion, which led to the cross, then we can truly say, "Now I have begun."

Day after day we accept our failure, but we accept it because of our knowledge of the victory of the Cross. God has given us our vocation, as He gave it to the small boy who contributed his few loaves and fishes to help feed the multitude, and which Jesus multiplied so that He fed five thousand people.

Loaves and Fishes

There can be no revolution without a theory of revolution, Peter Maurin quotes Lenin as saying. Action must be preceded by thought: There is such a thing as the heresy of good works, "these accursed occupations," as St. Bernard calls them, which keep people from thinking. To feed the hungry, clothe the naked, and shelter the harborless without also trying to change the social order so that people can feed, clothe, and shelter themselves, is just to apply palliatives. It is to show a lack of faith in one's fellows, their responsibilities as children of God, heirs of heaven

February 1945

Palliatives, when what we need is a revolution, beginning now. Each one of us can help start it. It is no use talking about how bored we are with the world. Let us not be escapists but admit that it is upon us. We are going to have it imposed upon us, or we're going to make it our own.

If we don't do something about it, the world may well say, "Why bring children into the world, the world being what it is?" We bring them into it and start giving them a vision of an integrated life so that they too can start fighting.

This fighting for a cause is part of the zest of life. Fr. Damasus said once at one of our retreats, that people seemed to have lost that zest for life, that appreciation of the value of life, the gift of life. It is a fundamental thing. Helene Iswolsky in a lecture on Dostoevsky at the Catholic Worker last month, said that he was marked by that love for life. He had almost been shot once. He had been lined up with other prisoners and all but lost his life. From then on he had such a love for life that it glowed forth in all his writings.

But how can one have a zest for life under such conditions as those we live in at 115 Mott Street? How can that laundry worker down the street, working in his steamy hell of a basement all day, wake each morning to a zest for life?

The whole retreat movement is to teach people to "meditate in their hearts," to start to think of these things, to make a beginning, to go out and start to love God in all the little things of every day, to so make one's life and one's children's life a sample of heaven, a beginning of heaven.

The retreats are to build up a desire, a knowledge of what to desire. "Make me desire to walk in the way of Thy commandments." Daniel was a man of "desires." Our Lord is called "the desire of the everlasting hills."

Yes, we must write of these things, of the love of God and the love of His creatures, man and beast, and plant and stone.

June 1948

People Need Disturbing

When it is said that we disturb people too much by the words pacifism and anarchism, I can only think that people need to be disturbed, that their consciences need to be aroused, that they do indeed need to look into their work, and study new techniques of love and poverty and suffering for each other. Of course the remedies are drastic, but then too the evil is a terrible one and we are all involved, we are all guilty, and most certainly we are all going to suffer. The fact that we have "the faith," that we go to the sacraments, is not enough. "Inasmuch as ye have done it unto the least of these my brethren, ye have done it unto me" with napalm, nerve gas, our hydrogen bomb, our "new look."

Each one of us must make our decisions as to what he should do, each one must examine his conscience and beg God for strength. Should one register for the draft? Should one accept conscientious objector status in the army or out of it, taking advantage of the exceptions allowed, but accepting the fact of the draft? Should one pay tax which supports this gigantic program?

I realize how difficult this is to decide. Sometimes one can only make a gesture of protest. It is not for anyone to judge his fellow man on how far he can go in resisting participation in preparation for war. In the very works of mercy which we are performing, we at the Catholic Worker are being aided by those who earn what they do only because they pay income tax for war. Oh yes, the editors of *The Catholic Worker* know only too well how far we too are involved in the city of this world.

We are one world and all men are brothers. We must pray to learn to love, to have faith in love.

Lord I believe, help thou my unbelief; take away my heart of stone and give me a heart of flesh; in thee have I hoped, let me never be confounded.

April 1954

What Is to Be Done?

When a mother, a housewife, asks what she can do, one can only point to the way of St. Thérèse, that little way, so much misunderstood and so much despised. She did all for the love of God, even to putting up with the irritation in herself caused by the proximity of a nervous nun. She began with working for peace in her own heart, and willing to love where love was difficult, and so she grew in love, and increased the sum total of love in the world, not to speak of peace.

Newman wrote: "Let us but raise the level of religion in our hearts, and it will rise in the world. He who attempts to set up God's kingdom in his heart, furthers it in the world." And this goes for the priest, too, wherever he is, whether he deals with the problem of war or with poverty. He may write and speak, but he needs to study the little way, which is all that is available to the poor, and the only alternative to the mass approach of the State. But as Pope John told the pilgrimage of women, Mothers for Peace, the seventy-five of us who went over to Rome to thank him for his encyclical *Pacem in Terris,* just the month before his death, "the beginnings of peace are in your own hearts, in your own families, schoolrooms, offices, parishes, and neighborhoods."

It is working from the ground up, from the poverty of the stable, in work as at Nazareth, and also in going from town to town, as in the public life of Jesus two thousand years ago. And since a thousand years are as one day, and

Christianity is but two days old, let us take heart and start now.

December 1965

Now We Have Begun

It seems to me that we must begin to equal a little bit the courage of the Communists. One of the ways my Communist friends taunt me is by saying, in effect, "People who are religious believe in everlasting life, and yet look how cowardly they are. And we who believe only in this life, see how hard we work and how much we sacrifice. We are not trying to enjoy all this and heaven too. We are willing to give up our life in order to save it."

There is really no answer to this kind of taunt. When I was in Cuba in September 1962, I witnessed what a Franciscan priest, Hervé Chaigne, has called an "exemplary" revolution. I felt that it was an example to us in zeal, in idealism and in self-sacrifice and that unless we began to approach in our profession of Christianity some of this zeal of the Communists, we weren't going to get anywhere. But we have to go ahead and think in terms of a third way, not just those two alternatives, capitalism or communism, or my country or the fellowship of all men. We have to begin to see what Christianity really is, that "our God is a living fire; though He slay me yet will I trust Him." We have to think in terms of the Beatitudes and the Sermon on the Mount and have this readiness to suffer. "We have not yet resisted unto blood." We have not yet loved our neighbor with the kind of love that is a precept to the extent of laying down our life for him. And our life very often means our money, money that we have sweated for; it means our bread, our daily living, our rent, our clothes. We haven't shown ourselves ready to lay down our life. This is a new precept, it is a new way, it is the new man we are supposed to become. I always comfort myself by saying that Christianity is only two days old (a thousand years are as one day in the sight of God) and so it is only a couple of days that are past and now it is about time we began to take these things literally, to begin tomorrow morning and say, "now I have begun."

April 1968

Penance

We certainly must have the long view into the future to see and realize the awakening of the masses of people throughout the world and the growth of a new vision among them of a world which is personalist and communitarian. *The great problem is: what means are to be used?*

Thank God we are not living in that time when Africa was divided between all the European powers, and England, France, and Holland dominated the Far East, when nobody knew or cared that their comfort in the West was built on the blood, sweat, and tears of toilers of the world.

The battle at home now is to conquer the bitterness, the sense of futility and despair that grows among the young and turns them to violence, a violence which is magnified by the press, the radio, and television. We lose sight of the poor people's cooperatives and boycotts, the conquest of bread, as Kropotkin called it, which goes on daily in Alabama, Mississippi, Louisiana, not to speak of California, Texas, and all the states where Mexicans have been imported for agricultural labor. The work of unionization, the formation of credit unions and cooperatives, especially cooperative housing, must go on, as must the work of building up hope and a sense in men of their own capacity for change, and for bringing about change. The only thing that keeps hope alive is work, and study must go with it, to keep one's hope and vision alive.

I could not help but think that just as we cannot love God whom we do not see unless we love our brother whom we do see, it followed that our faith in man (as he could be) should increase our faith in God and His ever-present aid. "I can do all things in Him who strengthens me." "Without Him I can do nothing." And this very small conversation made me pray the more.

But how can we show our love by war, by the extermination of our enemies? If we are followers of Christ, there is no room for speaking of the "just war." We have to remember that God loves all men, that God wills all men to be saved, that indeed all men are brothers. We must love the jailer as well as the one in prison. We must do that seemingly utterly impossible thing: love our enemy.

Penance seems to be ruled out today. One hears the Mass described as Sacrament, not as Sacrifice. But how are we to keep our courage unless the Cross, that mighty failure, is kept in view? Is the follower greater than his master? What attracts one in a Che Guevara and Ho Chi Minh is the hardships and the suffering they endured in living their lives of faith and hope. It is not the violence, the killing of one's enemies. A man is a man, and to hear him crying out in pain and anguish, whether he is friend or enemy, is to have one's heart torn in unutterable sorrow. The impulse to stand out against the State and go to jail rather than serve is an instinct for penance, to take on some of the suffering of the world, to share in it.

The thing is to recognize that not all are called, not all have the vocation, to demonstrate in this way, to fast, to endure the pain and long-drawn-out, nerve-racking suffering of prison life. We do what we can, and the whole field of all the works of mercy is open to us. There is a saying, "Do what you are doing." If you are a student, study, prepare, in order to give to others, and keep alive in yourselves, the vision of a new social order. All work, whether building, increasing food production, running credit unions, working in factories which produce for true human needs, working in the smallest of industries, the handcrafts—all these things can come under the heading of the works of mercy, which are the opposite of the works of war.

It is a penance to work, to give oneself to others, to endure the pinpricks of community living. One would certainly say on many occasions, "Give me a good thorough, frank outgoing war, rather than the sneak attacks, stabs in the back, sparring, detracting, defaming, hand to hand jockeying for position that goes on in offices and good works of all kinds, another and miserably petty kind of war." St. Paul said that "he died daily." This too is penance, to be taken cheerfully, joyfully, with the hope that our own faith and joy in believing will strengthen Chuck [Matthei] and all the others in jail.

So let us rejoice in our own petty sufferings and thank God we have a little penance to offer, in this holy season. "An injury to one is an injury to all," the Industrial Workers of the World proclaimed: So an act of love, a voluntary taking on oneself of some of the pain of the world, increases the courage and love and hope of all.

February 1969

FOLLY OF THE CROSS

St. Paul wrote that the gospel of Christ crucified was "foolishness to the gentiles." Dorothy frequently returned to this theme. Christ fulfilled his mission through apparent failure. This logic was indeed folly in the eyes of the world. The same was true for the message of nonviolence, the practice of voluntary poverty, the belief in a greater power disguised in what was apparently weak and insignificant, the conviction that love was more powerful than hate. All this was considered folly. And yet, at the same time, it was considered rational and logical to develop and prepare for the use of weapons that could kill hundreds of millions. In this light, Dorothy stated, "We confess to being fools, and wish that we were more so."

We are urging what is a seeming impossibility—a training in the use of nonviolent means of opposing injustice, servitude and a deprivation of the means of holding fast to the Faith. It is again the Folly of the Cross. But how else is the Word of God to be kept alive in the world? That Word is Love, and we are bidden to love God and to love one another. It is the whole law, it is all of life. Nothing else matters. Can we do this best in the midst of such horror as has been going on these past months by killing, or by offering our lives for our brothers?

June 1940

We confess to being fools and wish that we were more so. In the face of the approaching atom bomb test (and discussion of widespread radioactivity is giving people more and more of an excuse to get away from the philosophy of personalism and the doctrine of free will); in the face of an approaching maritime strike; in the face of bread shortages and housing shortages; in the face of the passing of the draft extension, teenagers included, we face the situation that there is nothing we can do for people except to love them.

What we would like to do is change the world—make it a little simpler for people to feed, clothe, and shelter themselves as God intended them to do. And to a certain extent, by fighting for better conditions, by crying out unceasingly for the rights of the workers, of the poor, of the destitute— the rights of the worthy and the unworthy poor in other words, we can to a certain extent change the world; we can work for the oasis, the little cell of joy and peace in a harried world. We can throw our pebble in the pond and be confident that its ever-widening circle will reach around the world.

We repeat, there is nothing that we can do but love, and dear God—please enlarge our hearts to love each other, to love our neighbor, to love our enemy as well as our friend.

June 1946

Unless the Seed Dies

Unless the seed fall into the ground and die, itself remaineth alone. But if it die it bringeth forth much fruit. So I don't expect any success in anything we are trying to do, either in getting out a paper, running houses of hospitality or farming groups, or retreat houses on the land. I expect that everything we do will be attended with human conflicts, and the suffering that goes with it, and that this suffering will water the seed to make it grow in the future. I expect that all our natural love for each other which is so warming and so encouraging and so much a reward of this kind of work and living, will be killed, put to death painfully by gossip, intrigue, suspicion, distrust, etc., and that this painful dying to self and the longing for the love of others will be rewarded by a tremendous increase of supernatural love amongst us all. I expect the most dangerous of sins cropping up amongst us, whether of sensuality or pride, it does not matter, but that the struggle will go on to such an extent that God will not let it hinder the work but that the work will go on, because that work is our suffering and our sanctification.

So rejoice in failures, rejoice in suffering!

January 1948

Fools for Christ

All our talks about peace and the weapons of the spirit are meaningless unless we try in every way to embrace *voluntary poverty* and not work in any position, any job that contributes to war, not to take any job whose pay comes from the fear of war, of the atom bomb. We must give up our place in this world, sacrifice children, family, wife, mother, and embrace poverty, and then we will be laying down life itself.

And we will be considered *fools for Christ.* Our folly will be esteemed madness, and we will be lucky if we escape finally the psychopathic ward. We know—we have seen this judgment in ourselves and in others. The well-dressed man comes into the office, and he is given respect. The ragged, ill-clad, homeless one is the hobo, the bum. "Get in line there. Coffee line forms at six-thirty. Nothing to eat until four. No clothes today."

Peter Maurin, visiting our Buffalo house one time, showed his face inside the door and was so greeted. "Come back at five and have soup with the rest of the stiffs." And then the comment, "One of those New York bums came in this afternoon, said he was from the New York house."

May 1948, *On Pilgrimage*

All the Way to Heaven

We are not expecting utopia here on this earth. But God meant things to be much easier than we have made them. A man has a natural right to food, clothing, and shelter. A certain amount of goods is necessary to lead a good life. A family needs work as well as bread. Property is proper to man. We must keep repeating these things. Eternal life begins now. [*Quoting St. Catherine of Siena:*] "All the way to heaven is heaven, because He said, 'I am the Way.'" The

Cross is there of course, but "in the cross is joy of spirit." And love makes all things easy. If we are putting off the old man and putting on Christ, then we are walking in love, and love is what we all want. But it is hard to love, from the human standpoint and from the divine standpoint, in a two-room apartment. We are eminently practical, realistic.

June 1948, *On Pilgrimage*

Starting with Oneself

There are books to be read with prayer in order to achieve understanding. For instance, do you know what it is to have your person violated, taken hold of, dragged, thrown, stripped, and degraded? Jesus Christ knew these things and we view His way when we make the Stations of the Cross. These may seem extreme parallels, but St. Paul recalled that trial as "the Folly of the Cross," and so indirectly referred to Christ as the Fool of His time. He loved even to folly. He said we should forgive seventy times seven. He said to love your enemies. He told that foolish tale of the prodigal son, which if you stop to think of it, is madness and folly on the part of the old man who showed such a lack of appreciation for the sturdy qualities of the older son and contributed so to the delinquency of the younger. Why did he give him his inheritance, knowing his temperament and that he would spend it on drink and women? And then to forgive him, to fall on his neck and embrace him, to feast with him and spend more money on him! No doubt the youth fell again and again, and did the seventy times seven business work here? The folly of the Cross! The failure of the Cross!

I write these things because pacifism today seems just such folly. "What good does a handful of men do?" everyone asks. How does one man going on a hunger strike far away in a grey cell behind bars mean laying down his life for his brother? And what good does it do?

One always is alone in doing these things. The revolution starts with oneself.

April 1950

WHAT IS THE CATHOLIC WORKER?

In many articles and editorials, Dorothy outlined the "aims and purposes" of the Catholic Worker, including reasons behind the works of mercy, the houses of hospitality, voluntary poverty, the commitment to the cause of the workers, the belief in nonviolence, and the effort to build "a new world in the shell of the old." What was it all about? It was a sign pointing toward a different way, a prophetic voice crying in the wilderness, an effort to plant seeds for a new social order. In one of her last reflections, she called it a kind of school where young people find their vocation and learn to love with compassion and to overcome fear.

Poverty, Work, Obscurity

This is the foundation stone of The Catholic Worker movement. It is on this that we build. Because of love we embrace voluntary poverty and the Works of Mercy, those two means of showing our love for our fellows. There is not much sense to either of these techniques otherwise. It is the folly of the Cross. It is the wisdom given to little ones, to confound the wise. It is the little way St. Thérèse of Lisieux spoke of. . . .

We walk by faith and not by sight, as St. Paul said, and we see things through a glass darkly. But we do know that love fulfills the law and that love is the measure by which we shall be judged. So though we feed thousands every day, if we haven't love, we have accomplished nothing. We live with wayfarers and the lame, the halt and the blind, but if we just shelter them, feed them, and clothe them and do not love them, it is nothing. We go out on picket lines and distribute literature, to try to bring the message of Christ and His love to the workers who are lost to the Church, but if we work without love, it is in vain. Let us pray then that the love of God will increase in our hearts, and that this desire to love be strengthened in us.

May 1939

Aims and Purposes (1940)

For the sake of new readers, for the sake of men on our breadlines, for the sake of the employed and unemployed, the organized and unorganized workers, and also for the sake of ourselves, we must reiterate again and again what are our aims and purposes.

Together with the Works of Mercy, feeding, clothing, and sheltering our brothers, we must indoctrinate. We must "give reason for the faith that is in us." Otherwise we are scattered members of the Body of Christ, we are not "all members one of another." Otherwise, our religion is an opiate, for ourselves alone, for our comfort or for our individual safety or indifferent custom.

We cannot live alone. We cannot go to Heaven alone. Otherwise, as Péguy said, God will say to us, "Where are the others?"

If we do not keep indoctrinating, we lose the vision. And if we lose the vision, we become merely philanthropists, doling out palliatives.

The vision is this. We are working for "a new heaven and a new *earth*, wherein justice dwelleth." We are trying to say with action, "Thy will be done on *earth* as it is in heaven." We are working for a Christian social order.

We believe in the brotherhood of man and the Fatherhood of God. This teaching, the doctrine of the Mystical

Body of Christ, involves today the issue of unions (where men call each other brothers); it involves the racial question; it involves cooperatives, credit unions, crafts; it involves Houses of Hospitality and Farming Communes. It is with all these means that we can live as though we believed indeed that we are all members one of another, knowing that when "the health of one member suffers, the health of the whole body is lowered."

This work of ours toward a new heaven and a new earth shows a correlation between the material and the spiritual, and, of course, recognizes the primacy of the spiritual. Food for the body is not enough. There must be food for the soul. Hence the leaders of the work, and as many as we can induce to join us, must go daily to Mass, to receive food for the soul. And as our perceptions are quickened, and as we pray that our faith be increased, we will see Christ in each other, and we will not lose faith in those around us, no matter how stumbling their progress is. It is easier to have faith that God will support each House of Hospitality and Farming Commune and supply our needs in the way of food and money to pay bills, than it is to keep a strong, hearty, living faith in each individual around us—to see Christ in him. If we lose faith, if we stop the work of indoctrinating, we are in a way denying Christ again.

We must practice the presence of God. He said that when two or three are gathered together, there He is in the midst of them. He is with us in our kitchens, at our tables, on our breadlines, with our visitors, on our farms. When we pray for our material needs, it brings us close to His humanity. He, too, needed food and shelter. He, too, warmed His hands at a fire and lay down in a boat to sleep.

When we have spiritual reading at meals, when we have the rosary at night, when we have study groups, forums, when we go out to distribute literature at meetings, or sell it on the street corners, Christ is there with us. What we do is very little. But it is like the little boy with a few loaves and fishes. Christ took that little and increased it. He will do the rest. What we do is so little we may seem to be constantly failing. But so did He fail. He met with apparent failure on the Cross. But unless the seed fall into the earth and die, there is no harvest.

And why must we see results? Our work is to sow. Another generation will be reaping the harvest.

February 1940

Aims and Purposes (1943)

"Love is an exchange of gifts," St. Ignatius said. And we want to show our love for our brother, so that we can show our love for God; and the best way we can do it is to try to give him what we've got, in the way of food, clothing, and shelter; to give him what talents we possess by writing, drawing pictures, reminding each other of the love of God and the love of man. There is too little love in this world, too little tenderness.

How can we love God and kill our brother? How can we love our brother and kill him? How can we fulfill the Gospel precept to be perfect as our heavenly father is perfect; how can we follow the precept to love God when we kill our fellow man? How can war be compatible with such love?

Why do we write about cooperatives, credit unions, mutual aid? Because when we see what Christianity is, when we see the beauty of our faith—when we have gone through something analogous to a conversion, we see all things new, as St. Paul says. We look upon our work, our lives, and we say, "How do these things square with Christian teaching? Can we go on making money at the expense of our brother? Can we be profiteers, can we work on Wall Street? Can we go in for advertising which sets up false standards, which perverts the people, which fills their minds with meretricious desires, making the good sweet life of the Christian unpalatable?" If we wish to follow Christ, we will be workers like Jesus, like St. Joseph, like St. Paul. We will think of the dignity of labor, we will respect the worker, will bear our share of responsibility toward making that new social order wherein justice dwelleth, where people will have that certain amount of goods which St. Thomas says is necessary to lead a good life.

Why do we talk about houses of hospitality, breadlines, and farming communes and the necessity of taking care of our poorer brother? Because the greatest hypocrisy is this, to say to our brother in need, "Go, be now filled," and give him no bread.

How can we show our love for God except through our love for our brothers?

How can we cease to cry out against injustice and human misery?

We cannot talk of the love of God, the love of our neighbor without recognizing the dire need for penance. In a world in which such cruelty exists, in which men are so possessed, such a spirit cannot be cast out but by prayer and fasting. Our Lord Himself said so.

May 1943

An Exchange of Gifts

The Catholic Worker is like an inn by the side of the road, with travelers coming and going, staying a day or a month or years, and the travelers are workers and scholars, poets, politicians, propagandists. Perhaps I should say that St. Joseph's House of Hospitality is like that, but the fact is that people are attracted to the CW, to the publication itself, because of its ideas. Write about peace and freedom and people who want to work as pacifists and anarchists come wandering in and become part of a community. You write about the works of mercy, and people who want to perform them come to try to put into practice the things they read about in the lives of the saints. But to me, the best thing about the works of mercy is that they become mutual aid, people helping each other, cooking meals, going to market, peeling vegetables, washing clothes, or giving them out, making beds, putting people up. Love is an exchange of gifts, St. Ignatius said, so true charity, caritas, enters in and mutual aid means true justice.

June 1957

Love One Another

What we really are, and try to be, in all the Catholic Worker houses around the country, is a family—and gentleness and loving-kindness is the prevailing mood.

I wonder how many of our readers have read Knut Hamsun's book *Hunger*. Or remember the incident in James Baldwin's *Another Country* where a young lad almost sells himself for a hot meal, and a place to sleep.

There is a statue on top of my bookcase given to me by a young boy whom we took care of some years back. He had lived this life on the streets. To prevent such things, even for a time, is something. I. F. Stone in his recent *Weekly* commenting on the bomb tragedy on Eleventh Street, said, "Man himself is obsolete unless he can change. That change requires more altruism, more kindness, more—no one need to be ashamed to say it—more love."

Love shows itself in gentleness, in tenderness, and manifests itself physically in serving and accepting service from another. Hans Tunnesen, our Norwegian seaman cook, uses the word *gentle* as his highest form of praise. When he says a man is gentle, he makes us all realize how good a word that is.

We are, too, a community of need, rather than what sociologists call an "intentional community." When people ask us how long people stay with us, meaning "the poor" (although we are all poor), we say, "For life." One of the Works of Mercy is burying the dead, and we remember them all as we say Compline in the country, and Vespers in the city, each night. . . .

But, my God, what a long and painful process this is, and yet how powerful! How long enduring! . . .

The most effective action we can take is to try to conform our lives to the folly of the Cross, as St. Paul called it.

May 1970

A New Social Order

Why do we give so much attention in the Catholic Worker to such matters as the condition of workers, unions, boycotts? This month I have had several letters, written undoubtedly by sincere and pious people who want to think only of contributing to breadlines and immediate needs of the poor. "Please spend this money for bread," they will write, "not on propaganda."

Let me say here that the sight of a line of men, waiting for food, ragged, dirty, obviously "sleeping out" in empty buildings, is something that I never will get used to. It is a deep hurt and suffering that this is often all we have to give. Our houses will not hold any more men and women, nor do we have workers to care for them. Nor are there enough alternatives or services to take care of them. They are the wounded in the class struggle, men who have built the railroads, worked in the mines, on ships, and steel mills. They are men from prison, men from mental hospitals. And women too. They all are often simply the unemployed.

We will never stop, having "lines" at Catholic Worker

houses. As long as men keep coming to the door we will keep on preparing each day the food they need.

But I repeat—Breadlines are not enough, hospices are not enough. I know we will always have men on the road. But we need communities of work, land for the landless, true farming communes, cooperatives and credit unions. There is much that is wild, prophetic, and holy about our work—it is that which attracts the young who come to help us. But the heart hungers for that new social order wherein justice dwelleth.

January 1972

A School

"What is it all about—the Catholic Worker Movement?" It is, in a way, a school, a work camp, to which large-hearted, socially-conscious, young people come to find their vocation. After some months or years, they know most definitely what they want to do with their lives. Some go into medicine, nursing, law, teaching, farming, writing and publishing.

They learn not only to love, with compassion, but to overcome fear, that dangerous emotion that precipitates violence. They may go on feeling fear, but they know the means, they have grown in faith, to overcome it. "Lord, deliver us from the *fear* of our enemies." Not from our enemies, but from the fear of them.

March–April 1975

Postscript

Dorothy concluded her memoir, The Long Loneliness, *with this postscript.*

We were just sitting there talking when Peter Maurin came in.

We were just sitting there talking when lines of people began to form, saying, "We need bread." We could not say, "Go, be thou filled." If there were six small loaves and a few fishes, we had to divide them. There was always bread.

We were just sitting there talking and people moved in on us. Let those who can take it, take it. Some moved out and that made room for more. And somehow the walls expanded.

We were just sitting there talking and someone said, "Let's all go and live on a farm."

It was as casual as all that, I often think. It just came about. It just happened.

I found myself, a barren woman, the joyful mother of children. It is not easy always to be joyful, to keep in mind the duty of delight.

The most significant thing about the Catholic Worker is poverty, some say.

The most significant thing is community, others say. We are not alone anymore.

But the final word is love. At times it has been, in the

words of Father Zosima, a harsh and dreadful thing, and our very faith in love has been tried through fire.

We cannot love God unless we love each other. We know Him in the breaking of bread, and we know each other in the breaking of bread, and we are not alone anymore. Heaven is a banquet and life is a banquet, too, even with a crust, where there is companionship.

We have all known the long loneliness and we have learned that the only solution is love and that love comes with community.

It all happened while we sat there talking, and it is still going on.

The Long Loneliness